What Do You Do When You Marry The Wrong Rib? Coming From A Place Called There!

By: Dr. Kenneth DeWayne Grimble

Cover & Graphic Design by Jeremiah Silva

Kingdom Empowerment Network Group

Publisher:

P.O. Box 3002 Springfield, IL 62708

Library of Congress Control Number: TXu 1-840-455

ISBN10: 0981976921

ISBN-13: 978-0-9819769-2-1

ACKNOWLEDGEMENTS

The book entitled, "What Do You Do When You Marry The Wrong Rib? Coming from a place called there" is a must read master piece written by Archbishop Kenneth D. Grimble. Marriage according to God has been uniquely presented in this book. I personally recommend this book to Parents to instruct their children and to pastors to teach on matters of the home to their church members. I also recommend that every household in the united states should by it, read it, apply it to their marriage and your family will find favor with God. A sweet savor in the nostrils of God has been present in this book for you to read. The purpose of marriage is designed for an intimate relationship with Jesus, the bride of Christ and everyone this is married or desire to be married as husband and wife.

Michael Nicholson
Servant of God
San Diego, California

The book entitled, "What Do You Do When You Marry the Wrong Rib? Coming From A Place Called There! is a message that really touches the heart of God in this awesome work. This is a must read that every couple considering marriage needs to study together. With elegant language the Bishop reveals the very heart of the Father concerning the joining of His children together. Marriage is the most important earthly relationship that we will ever engage in and this information is essential to getting the fullest potential out of your marriage relationship. There is understanding about the roles of husbands and wives and foundational truths that will forever impact your relationship!

Vander L. Williams
Senior Pastor-Kingdom Citizens Christian Center
Lillington, NC

The book entitled, "What Do You Do When You Marry The Wrong Rib? Coming from a place called there! is simply a must read for everyone. Dr. Kenneth D. Grimble is a profound teacher who God has used extensively to give spiritual guidance, mentor couples who are considering marriage as well as those who are already married. In his latest book, he has given intricate details of things that should be considered before a couple stands before God and take those vows. While identifying details of the underlying issues of failed marriage in general, he curtails that the world would be spiritually alert once it understands the significance of matrimony. This book is power packed with wisdom from God himself. The explosive concepts with principles if followed, will build restore and change any broken relationship.

Prophet Eric James
Shunammitte International Christian Center, Inc
Fayetteville, NC

ENDORSEMENTS

The book entitled, "What Do You Do When You Marry The Wrong Rib? Coming From A Place Called There!" is a must read for all who ponder, anticipate or intend to get married. Whatever stage you are in life, there are some wisdom nuggets in this book. Proverbs 1:7 says, "The Fear of the Lord is the beginning of wisdom" Archbishop Kenneth D. Grimble has allow himself to be used by God as an anointed ready pen writer for the beautiful journey of Holy Sacred Matrimony. This anointed read will help you regardless of your stage in life. Whatever status you are in be it single, divorced, newly engaged or about to embark in, this read will help you to avoid the many pitfalls, snares, traps, deceits and pain of being unequally yoked to the wrong rib that God has not chosen for you. As you read this timely word, it will bless you tremendously. Get your copy of this awesome book in What Do You Do When You Marry The Wrong Rib? Coming From A Place Called There!

Prophetess Elaine Jackson
Senior Leader of Prayerway Healing and Deliverance International Ministries, Inc
Statesboro, Georgia

The book entitled, "What Do You Do When You Marry The Wrong Rib? Coming From A Place Called There! is a must read book for the world and the body of Christ. After 51 years of marriage an no intimate knowledge of any other woman, I wish that I had this book prior to my marriage filled with nuggets of knowledge, wisdom, and understanding, Archbishop Kenneth D. Grimble is a skilled surgeon in the word of God and he has written this master piece that could surgically repair your marriage. This power packed book will change your future. Read it, understand it, live it and receive it. Your tomorrow will be greater than your yesterday, You will never regret reading this book for it will fill you with joy.

Archbishop Clarence Davis Sr.
Joy Cathedral
Chief Apostle & Presiding Prelate

DEDICATION

I want to dedicate this book to first and foremost to my wife and partner in faith Lady Diane Grimble. She believed in me and stuck by my side when I know that she should have taken the first flight out. My wife has been a source of strength that propelled me to push when everything in me said to give up and quit.

Lady Diane Grimble, I not only dedicate this book to you but also I also dedicate my life to you.......you are a wonderful friend, drill instructor, lover, wife and leader in the Kingdom of our Lord God.

I also dedicate this book to my mother, the late Bessie N. Grimble who was a pillar of strength, wisdom, knowledge and kindness in all the days of her life.

I dedicate this book to my father, Herb, brother, Kelvin, aunt, Jennie, my mother-in-law, Juanita.

I dedicate this book to my daughter Amber, two sons Antawn & Marvel.

I dedicate this book to my cousins Ricky, Harold, Lamont, Jeff, Felicia, Keisha...(too many to list).

I dedicate this book to my spiritual sons and daughters.

I dedicate this book to my spiritual father Archbishop Willie Bolden.

I dedicate this book to my spiritual mother, Apostle Dr. Polly Elliot.

I dedicate this book to my friends, associates and my enemies dedicate this book to all my professors, instructors and teachers and spiritual leaders.

Each member of my family that have played a role in my development as a Man of God that I became today.

I also want to say to my Grand Children, Ashton and Addison, you are a source of Joy and delight to me, Grand Daddy Loves you dearly.

CONTENTS

PREFACE

The writing of this book, entitled, *"What Do You Do When You Marry The Wrong Rib? Coming from a Place called there!"* The author's intent for this book was not written to instruct anyone to go out to get a divorce. However, the essence of the book is to prompt the next generation to seek to know God in an intimate way concerning the mate in which they desire to marry. Therefore, the premise of the book is to look at marriage in a more serious light and find qualifying factors to have a successful marriage. This book looks into the historical disposition of marriage in light of King Solomon and King David. The historical patterns of marriage cultivated a new breed of husband. While marriage was initially designed for only one man and one woman, there were patterns of marriage that were distorted by the enemy in good people.

The distorted perspective has left a plague in the institution of marriage. Because of the nuances that arise from the polluted lifestyles, marriages have lost their proclivity to maintain its biblical grip of righteousness. There are two keys figures such as King David and Kingdom Solomon in the bible had wives and concubines. This book will examine why so many find themselves with the wrong rib or the wrong mate. What is this lingering notion that allows men or women to feel a need for multiple partners? What are the motives for these marriages? Did God join them together? If not, does God scripturally bind you to the marriage once it has become clear that the marriage was entered with impure motives? In other words, God knows the heart of both candidates for marriage. Because God ability to know the true motives for the intent of marriage, the interconnection is usually with unclean motives. Some people get married as a result of the defining moment of making the relationship legitimate. However, the actions of the couple don't understand the underlying factors of being in a relationship without Gods input or endorsement. When self or flesh chooses to get married without the promptings of God, the ensuing question comes to the forefront. Are we bound to stay in the marriage in which God did not endorse? While there is evidence that some people will only marry someone for position, prestige or prosperity, there are special cases where the love of God is truly abound. The entertainment and Sports industry have compiled many divorces and remarriages with a blink of an eye. From an outsider looking in, there appears to be a great deal of money being exchanged and new address to say the least.

Since many of the professional athletes have extremely high salaries, there is a tendency for a group of women affectionately called gold diggers that set a course to secure their future with these sports celebrities. Some savvy movie stars and professional athletes use prenuptial agreements as evidence of their pending spouse's intent to marry for love and not purely for the money. Whether it is the sporting star, the movie star, the lawyer or doctor, there have always been groupies hanging around willing to do anything to latch on to the wealthy practitioners'.

INTRODUCTION

The institution of marriage and the divorce decree were both created by God to serve in His designated purpose for his designated purpose. While it may appear to be perplexing to understand the nature of marriage, there is also its antithesis in the subject of divorce. The true intent in which divorce was created is not really clear in a much wider span than we think. However, it is very clear that God does not like that nature in which divorce is being used in the world today. Every male thinks that the woman they marry is a proverbs 31 woman but later finds that she is an odious woman. The difference between the two is life changing, thought provoking and quite possibly could keep you out of heaven. The intent of this written discourse is not to malign women or the chosen woman that the male reader chooses to marry. Wisdom is crying out for true marriages to come forth. Solomon shared some great wisdom in proverbs 21:19, "It is better to dwell in the wilderness than with a contentious and an angry woman." What is a contentious woman? One with a disposition to contend with and who always argues, criticizes, disagrees, opposes, or questions you relentlessly. The distinction of the proverbs 31 woman and the odious woman has directly impacted our culture in a monumental way.

As we delve further into this process, you will see that the odious wife is an adverse, incomplete and infamous version of the proverbs 31 woman. It is an altruistic effort of some women to be imitators of the biblically based depiction of a true expression woman after the heart of God. She is well balanced, esteemed and highly recognized by others as well as her children who call her blessed. Let us move through these pages and examine how the nature of marriage has been impacted by ungodly motives being camouflaged by impure directives. The answer will shed light as to why so many marriages in the church as well as outside have ended in divorce. Furthermore, the mindset of many pretender's have been manipulated to stay in marriages that have been violated by prognosticators of those who lived a life uncommitted and unfaithful to their families and placed in a renewed level of infidelity.

CHAPTER 1
MARRIAGE UNDER THE MICROSCOPE

The Lord God makes a strong affirmation for the Institution of marriage. In the same inference, he looks at the church as the bride and he is the bride groom. Just as the church is the epitome of a wedding about to take place, so it is that we are to model the church as the institution of marriage. If we were to get a glimpse of the church in its present stage, we would be perplexed at the present disposition of a bride. For those who are married, God treats the church as his soon- to- be bride. The similarity is by no coincidence because everything he created is designed for his purpose and pleasure.

According to Hebrews 13:4 the Bible says," marriage is honourable in all, and the bed undefiled, but whoremongers and adulterers God will Judge." Apostle Paul informs the reader that marriage is honorable in the eyesight of God and the bed is undefiled. The latter part of this text implies the bed to be undefiled. More than likely, it implies that two adults can engage in unlimited boundaries to please one another. While many will try to regulate what goes on between a husband and wife, it should be a discussion between the two prior to marriage as to what should or should not be done. It is because of outside influences that many marriages are in trouble in our society. No one can measure the obstacles that incur in their marriage and apply it to another.

Every individual is accountable to God and not the opinions of another couple. While it is good to have wise counsel, it is also essential that the marriage be established where both spouses have an intimate relationship with the true and almighty God. According to I Corinthians 7:14, "For the unbelieving husband is sanctified by the wife, and the unbelieving wife is sanctified by the husband else where your children unclean; but now are they holy." In other words, the scripture indicates that the unbelieving husband is sanctified by the wife and the unbelieving wife is cleansed by the sanctified husband. Having children is supposed to be a blessing to a union in matrimony. However, the union should be with a husband and wife as opposed to man and woman experiencing sex. There are so many people who have been hoodwinked into to thinking that sex outside of marriage is approved by God.

Unfortunately, this is not the case in the pavilion of Glory as it should not be the case in earth realm as well. The earth realm is the practical dimension of the flesh that the inhabitants operate within this sphere. The mere fact that many don't understand the war between the flesh and the spirit. The flesh was never designed to be saved due to the fall from grace. Therefore, God has required his inhabitants to exercise temperance. The carnality of mankind seeks to be appeased because it in itself cannot be saved. It takes temperance of mankind to put the flesh under subjection. Because of the wide latitude of sexual revolution, there seems to be a relaxed behavior regarding the subject of marriage. The main stanza for many is that marriage is only a piece of paper. In a magical sense of expression, the marriage license is physical validation of the marriage. This is done by justice of the peace or an ordained clergy of a viable ministry or Church.

The biggest mistake that many people avoid before getting married is the need to undertake an extensive course marriage counseling. Many things are learned during this process and should be brought to the attention of the couple prior to the ceremony. There are some crucial issues that need to be brought to light and discussed with great intensity in either an open forum or in separate meetings with each candidate individually. The clergy also plays a vital role in determining whether or not the couple is ready for marriage mentally, spiritual or financially. Furthermore, it is essential that all questions should be brought to light as such things as sex, child rearing, finances, living arrangements, medical conditions or genuine expectations from each party considering marriage.

Subtle things are often overlooked by both parties because they are so eager to get married. In all the excitement, they just want the ceremony to be over with so that they can exercise one of many privileges that are biblically accessible and pleasing to God through matrimony. There are many that decide against the biblical approach to marriage and begin living together according to their own understanding. The term most often used by the church is coined "shacking". This approach is characterized as an "ungodly" trial run to see how the couple can cope with living together without the obligation and definitive mandate that marriage incurs. While there are some benefits to this approach, they are minimally recognized and frowned upon because of the unbiblical reality. Moreover, this approach is frowned upon by God because he does not need any help. It comes down to believing and displaying trust in God. They indicated that they planned to get married but wanted to save up money together and plan for the wedding at a later date.

However, there is strong indication that proves that these individual seldom follow through with their wedding plans. In actuality, the approach gives a close up perspective that reveals that the two were not compatible and ended up breaking off their relationship. While everyone that plans to get married is confident that the present aspirant is the real deal, they end up being relieved to know that their plans were halted. Many find out after living together without being married to that the person. This relationship ends abruptly and the two stray so far apart because they moved ahead of God to do their own agenda. As a result of this decision, the ark of safety was lifted and released a plethora demons as a result of this major decision. The plans of Gods for marriage is based on the strength of biblical principles towards matrimony requiring both parties to trust God and the sacredness of marriage.

While marriage is a beautiful institution, we must understand that being married is only beautiful when the two candidates were divinely connected by God. Many get married out of obligation rather than out of the sentiments of Gods word and his divine splendor. Each candidate desiring to get marriage must examine for themselves and embrace a true understanding of God's word relative to their roles in the process. In today's society, there is too much confusion with regard to role of the husband and wife. It appears that many women feel that they are equal in terms to the role of their husband because they bring something to the table.

Although it is true that they are equal in Gods eyesight from a creatorship standpoint, there is drastic difference between the role of a husband and the wife. If we were to look at the strong deduction for couples to properly be trained for their roles as husband and wife, the approach to marriage would be different. There is a distinct different from a proverbs 31 wife and an odious wife. (We will discuss the differences later on in the book). Our creator has given us a blue print for marriage but the plan is often times overlooked for self seeking individuals to get their own way. In other words, the roles within plans of God are shoved in the endless vault. The institution of marriage is current on a path that has been on a downward spiraling affect. If marriages have been negatively impacted, one would think that the divorce rate of marriages would be higher in the world. The alarming increase in failed marriages have piled up and amassed an all time high inside the church. The misleading notion is that the rate of divorces in the church negatively impacted by those who only attend church.

It should not be characterized that the statistics are married because there is an assumption that attending by religious standards is indicative to being part of the church by relationship. The numbers are staggering but should be taken or thought to be inaccurate as to the real total. However, the implication is very damaging due to the impact of its intent. Furthermore, we must see the awkward hands of the devil and his diabolical mission to keep the church attendees from connecting through divine intervention. The church is supposed to emulate the decorum of a bride. In any event, the view of the church as a bride would be half dressed as a harlot and half dressed as a celebrity super star model. The combined view would more likely be viewed like a prostitute wearing a wedding dress.

The portrait of the church would be more like those with one foot in the church and the other foot deeply imbedded in the world. There is a tendency for the world to treat the church with new trends that prohibit the church from moving beyond the dead skin of religion. There are creative reasons for snakes to shed skin. The same sentiments are identical for demons and devils. However, the religious church does not know how to function with Gods intended blue print. Because the world is an enemy to God, there must be a further push to catapult the church into the next dimension. While this current paradigm shift in the church would make an immediate impact, there has to be renewed mindset to stop resisting truth. Unless the true church redeem the time, the institution of marriage is doomed.

Because the view from the world and the church are skewed, the standards and respect for the word of God must be honored. The Bible says in St. John 9:5, "As long as I am in the world, I am the light of the world." The writer of this book, Apostle John, is making a strong declaration of the significance of Gods illuminating existence. The reason for the damages to marriages is because the candidates getting married have no spiritual enlightenment or ability to hear from God. When the vessel recognize the inability to hear or understand the spiritual nuggets in reading the word of God, they move on their own free will. This is a typical response from a person who has a free will to do as he desires. This individual does not only have information about God but they also fail to testify that they have a personal relationship with God.

The Bible says in St. John 10:4-5, "And when he putteth forth his own sheep, he goeth before them, and the sheep follow him: for they know his voice. And a Stranger will they not follow, but will flee from him: for they know not the voice of strangers." Furthermore, Apostle John states in St. John 10:16, "And other sheep I have, which are not of this fold: them also I must bring, and they shall hear my voice; and there shall be one fold, and one shepherd." The emphasis in the proceeding text is that they could only follow instructions with the ability to hear clear spiritually because they had the capacity to tune into his frequency. The propensity to hear is to have the ability to tune in onto the right frequency for which carnal Christians are unable to access. Therefore, they go ahead and get married for all the wrong reasons. On many occasions, the marriage last six months to two years before a divorce reached. The Bible says in St. John 9:39, "And Jesus said, "For judgment I come into this world that they which see not might see; and they which see might be made blind. John clearly illustrates in the above mentioned text that many claim to know God shall not see or hear from him.

However, there are some who spend the time in prayer, life the life of righteous and have the ability without pressing forward for fear. As a result, many of the church members avoid the spiritual development required to guard their destinies and move into their flesh. The motives are only justified because they desire to move in their flesh. So, they get married to satisfy their quest for intimacy and end up finding out that they were incapable outside of the bedroom. They selected their mate based on personal criteria rather than waiting on God to give them what he desired for them. Many choose to embrace Gods permissive will rather than his perfect will.

The significance of marriage is a mystery that God reveals the answers to those who will get in tune, in his presence and in his word. We must remember that God honors marriage and he endorses the benefits that those who embrace his word and will. Every now and then, the devil gains access through an ungodly portal. The institution of marriage is under the most pivotal platform since the eons of time. The greatest attack has now come when the devil has invaded the minds of his creation and some of his children with a homosexual agenda. The enemies' effort to use sexual promiscuity to gain access through a ungodly portal to embrace this abominable act. This act has been erroneously cast into the same category as sin. Moreover, the world has placed an undo burden on the church with its allowance of the world to take this abominable act and place as just mere sin.

Furthermore, the time has come for a massive launch to attempt to redefine the institution of marriage to include this abominable act in the name of love. This campaign stands to affect generations to come because it has aligned against God and against his divine blue print. The world's effort to embrace this notorious act in order to fit into plans of the world instead of the plans already prepared by God. While the world continues to open doors for demonic access points, there is an authority by the word and its power to send the devil back to the pit of hell.

This authority can only be accessed when the incumbents are empowered by his spirit, by his word and by is power which will grant them access. The enemy has tricked so many of the present day church attendee's to think they have access to power to deter the enemy from being effective in its demonic campaign.

Just as the enemy attempted in Acts 19 where the vagabond Jews attempted to cast out a devil without having the divine power or with being equipped or authorized to walk in believers authority. Remember, a devil has no authority to cast out itself. Only those who walk in righteousness can gain access to authority to cast out devils. Apostle Paul illustrated so clearly that there is a price to pay when believers are not properly prepared in spiritual warfare. According to Acts 19:13-15, "Then certain of the vagabond Jews, exorcists, took upon themselves to call over them which had evil spirits the name of the Lord Jesus, saying, We adjure you by Jesus whom Paul preacheth. And there were seven sons of one Sceva, a Jew and chief of the priests, which did so. And the evil spirit answered and said, Jesus I know and Paul I know, but who are ye?" It is clear that playing or mimicking the power of God can cause you to shorten your life.

You must be connected to God through his word and his power. The redefine the institution of marriage to allow two men or two women to unite in matrimony is evil in thought, deed and action. As for those who have attempted to redefine the institution, God will judge those who participate in this demonic endeavors. Within the creative nature of Gods superior power, the inhabitants of society and mankind have decided to go against the core of its unique design. In a nutshell, this is an emphatic reason of the abatement of the significance of the liturgy of abomination. In other words, God designed everything for his pleasure and purpose. He did not design men to be intimate with men nor women to be intimate with women sexually. This warped mentality has carried over to the minds of society and has slipped into the lifestyle of some churches.

Although the acceptance of this lifestyle as part of God's creative plan is an abatement from the blue print of truth, this nation is about to undertake the greatest crime against God's creative nature. Whenever truth is aborted, it is true sign for a door for the enemy to gain access. While the world does not believe that the devil exists, they do realize when these arsenal of attacks where killing innocent men, women, boys and girls are signs of the devil. These random killings are increasing at a monumental rate and perhaps a sign of the time of a demonic invasion. This is not a secret because the body of Christ has been warned. Many in the Church, including its church leaders, have allowed their spiritual ears to become dull. This would indicate why so many leaders can't hear from God in this hour. This pattern of thinking will hinder the bride of Christ from reaching its full potential. Consequently, this will nullify the resurrection of the true bride from being manifested. Thus, it will delay and deter the true bride from receiving her husband and the greatest marriage ceremony in the eons of time.

CHAPTER 2
THE FALLACY OF DATING

The purposed effort of building a strong relationship for those contemplating marriage was to assist in developing a better assessment of the potential candidate for marriage. Although the efforts have failed miserably, the candidates often find themselves in a perplexing stanza because they begin to enjoy the pleasure of having a variety of choice candidates to date. The agenda seemingly gets lost in the shuffle because the pursuer has begun to slip into deep water. The dating game becomes more of an opportunity to delve into an oasis of pleasure. This method of thinking is truly a lopsided venue of deception. With that being whispered, the original intent has been locked in a back burner vault. Needless to say, the great effort has taken a new twist and created a bridge from its original intent of finding the right mate. In modern times, there seems to be quagmire of questions in entering in the dating arena. What factors play a role is finding the divinely ordained spouse? Let's say the puddle of candidates is too small for a true assortment? Imagine that their true mate is in another state or geographic location?

Will the limitations be drawn if the selections are limited to my local venue? The circumstances for connecting can be as vivid as an individual that may attend college in a nearby or far location. It could be a connection stirred by an encounter with someone who may be in medical school in your local city. The endless possibilities are truly rare in the spectrum of divine encounters. People meet at business meetings, conventions, in stores, in the air port, in conferences and a host of other potential locations. It is just a myriad of places that could be a portal of candidates to build friendships that could move into a relationship resulting in marriage.

Although marriage is the decisive goal to the right person, there seems to be erroneous standards that have been set by generations from a poor thinking pattern. Some parents have spent years molding their children to marry for money. While it is true that some do marry for the convenience of financial security, they find quickly that their happiness was sacrificed for financial gain. Because times have changed and individuals are much smarter, there are those who would consider marriage with a prenuptial agreement. This agreement gives details of the marriage in regard to both parties that indicate strict details of distribution of assets if the marriage fails. This details include conditions while marriage and parameters of income distribution should the marriage end. This agreement is signed before the marriage takes place and shall be enforced should they decide to divorce.

Now the person cannot consider any option outside the marriage because they have signed an agreement that basically states as long as you are married to them you can live in this accustomed lifestyle. If you choose to leave the marriage, you will only take what you brought into the marriage. The conveniences that exist could be considered monumental because as soon as you shut the door on the marriage you digress to the point where you started. It is a heavy price to pay for those who consider marrying someone rich instead of marrying someone for divine love. The consuming notion of getting married only for financial security could lead to an unfulfilling life. Some will value the lifestyle over the opportunity for their true love to take root. Before you look at the portfolio, you should find out what type of person it is that you desire to be connected. Does this person display characteristics of control, abuse or double dealing? Some feel that their wealth entitles them to multiple relationships.

Can you live with a person that may feel that his or her wealth entitles them to engage in a casual affair? The historical precedent for arranging marriages has had a drastic impact on our society. During these times, financial estates were established and as a result they formed a business alliance uniting their children in marriage. It appears that love had not been the ultimate factor in these marriages. Furthermore, it appears that these marriages were a convenience or sacrifice for the family estate. Can you imagine sleeping next to someone for the rest of your life and not be in love with them. Now, the newly wed's having to go through the motion of pretending to love someone that they don't even know. They only got married to satisfy their family business dealings.

There are times when these individuals have had to relinquish relationships built on love and affections to satisfy their family obligations. This is clearly a case where one could question, "What Does Love have to do with it?" They continue this façade of a marriage as a duty and they have children that come as a result of a loveless relationship. It is a wonder to the eyes of the masses as to what is an authentic marriage based primarily on the perception presented. The pattern of marriage is a biblical concept that epitomized the relationship between God as the groom and the church serves as the body. Because of the nature of dating, the marriage ceremony is furthermore delayed or put on the shelf for the purpose of matrimony. Premarital sex has created another problem in the marriage because the relationship is tainted by the curse of premarital sex.

Many of the practitioners don't see the problem with having sex before marriage.

Furthermore, they have developed this standard that they must be compatible sexually before they will entertain marrying anyone. Sexual compatibility has been polluted by a diabolical agenda of the devil that promotes this deviation from the norm. Since the days of nimrod and his sexual encounter with his mother-in-law, there has been a gateway opened by the devil that allowed the enemy access into relationship. The doorway has not been shut to this spirit and as a result it continues to bombard the lives of those who are either in a relationship or in a marriage. The attitude of those courting or dating is tainted to feel a sense of entitlement for a sexual relationship as a measuring tool for the possibility of marriage.

The problem with this method of assessment is that they don't have an adequate measuring tool to bring value to the equation. How do you assess sexual compatibility? In a nutshell, this is just an opportunity to justify establishing an unholy alliance. Sex, outside of marriage, is a sin against their own bodies and a sin against God. The consequence of sex before marriage is very dangerous and severe. Demons are granted unlimited access to the incumbents innermost mortal soul due to the violation of sexual intercourse prior to marriage. This violation of a man and women having sex produces an ungodly soul tie. The plethora of spirits mingling inwardly due to the bridge of despair. In other words, each sexual encounter brings the couple into a oneness that is not easily severed. With that being said, the damage is done even if the couple never engage in intercourse again. The disparity between dating and courtship has a immeasurable difference in meaning. From the world standpoint, they are more accustomed with the term dating.

However, the church does not believe literally in the term dating. The term more acceptable to the church is courtship. The purpose of courtship is designed to prepare for marriage. On the other hand, dating is a term used to develop friendship. This friendship could be a long term relationship that may not necessarily end in marriage. This would be a devastating blow because a great deal of time has been invested into building the relationship. Because of the daggers' of dating relationships, there is a tendency to become codependent on a person's attention and a reluctance to let them go because of the fear of being alone. There is an atrocity brewing regarding a new wave of malodorous thinking. This philosophical methodology purports that some women have made it easy for men to drop in for an occasional sexual drive by state of mind.

It is apparent that more women would rather have a piece of a man than none at all. This mindset has created a portal of access into the church. Many spouses have opened a doorway to cheat at their leisure. They only stay in the marriage for the children and personal assets. They both agree to remain in the marriage for the sake of the children and to hold leverage on the financial assets attained but they have an open relationship to see others on a intimate basis.   It is truly apparent the most people do not honor their martial vows. Contrary to popular beliefs, the value of honoring the marital vow has dissipated drastically to a mere existence. The sacred vows of marriage have lost its significance humanly speaking.

Nevertheless, the spiritual meaning shall never deviate from the word of God. In other words, the word married does not mean anything to those who feel that they want to engage into an adulterous relationship. The devil has pushed this agenda to the point that more people are pondering if it is worth it to get married. In spite of this method of inserting doubt, the institution of marriage is a truly beautiful experience when it is with the right person.   Though marriage was designed to be complementary between a husband and wife, it has turned into a portal of competitive and combative altercations. Although there are those who engage in relationships that are either lesbian's or homosexuals, the subject matter is so vast to mention but often hidden in the cracks of the chronicles. This agenda has also violated scripture to the point that there is no fear of God.

Needless to say, God will have the last say about this unbiblical lifestyle. Furthermore, efforts have been purported to legitimize this lifestyle. In the scope of legitimacy, this lifestyle might be accepted by some but the truth of the matter is that it is not accepted by God.   As some would like to deviate from the true pattern of scripture, God created him male and female to bond in matrimony in the beauty of righteousness. The reference here is permeated with the institution of marriage. He did not created this institution for two males to bond nor two females to bond.

This discourse has placed an enormous enlightenment in the devils plight to attempt to redefine God's definition of courtship. The big shift in the matter is contributed to gaining clarity in the process as it relates to development. The expression of the three stage of the tabernacle is quite clear.

The outer court is associated with the initial phase of friendship. This ground breaking area is suited for establishment of an association. The premise of an access portal will be determined if the association will move to the next level. There is times that no forward progress or advancement shall take place. The inner court is comprised of a different dimension where two individuals have made advancement from the first phase and moved into a relationship basis. Within this area, there are dialogues and distinct conversation relative to the possibilities of a long term relationship. The two begin to access the intention of this relationship and move into the decision to seek the lord for more direction. Within this arena, the two relationship constituents begin to think of questions about marriage. Once the two have answered all their questions, they will begin to seek God for instructions as to their next move. The holy of hollies is an ultimate pinnacle for two people that have been divinely connected.

They have entered into a dimension where courtship is the epitome of their existence. They were made for this level of intimacy and shall not be mistaken for sex. The misunderstanding has a drastically impacted the nature of relating. It appears that the need for sex has handicapped fruitful relationship due primarily the curse of sin. Because these privileges were earmarked for those who entered into matrimony, this creates a monotonous euphoria for those who choose not to honor God requirements for the Kingdom of God. The out pouring of demonic overtures have infiltrated the institution of marriage to further the diabolical agenda to undermine the word of God. As indicated in previous chapters, the story of King Solomon had created a platform for devious thinking because he had three hundred concubines. In some cultures, they were considered live-in girl friends that served as a bond slave to her master.

The concept of concubines is still considered very vague in its disposition. While the nature of concubine is considered expansive in different culture, there are some that are treated like a wife but they have no claim to legitimacy. If a child is born, the child would be raised as if it was their master's wife's child. The diary of prostitution have been promulgated from this disposition. The concubine receives a home to live in to serve the wife and her master at their will. This concept is nothing more than a free slave that will provided room and board for sexual favors of the master when his wife is not available. This could have been a door opened to the nature of prostitution and the pimp. The pimp is the caregiver for the prostitute and

he receives compensation for work performed by the girls listed in his stable. The stable consist of young and old single girls that are trafficked from state to state selling their bodies for monetary gain. Each of the girls has been promised to be their pimp's main girl. However, they have been tricked into this life as prostitute. The dating game has allowed a demonic access portal to serve as a facilitator to make a lot of money off of these girls. The exchange is a place to stay and a minimum amount of money to live on.

CHAPTER 3
MARRIED TO JESUS CHRIST NOT A BUILDING MADE BY HANDS

The bible declares in Matthew 28:16-20 "Then the eleven disciples went away into Galilee, into a mountain where Jesus had appointed them. And when they saw him, they worshiped him: but some doubted. And Jesus came and spake unto them, saying, all power is given unto me in heaven and in earth. Go ye therefore, and teach all nations, baptizing them in the name of the Father, and the Son, and of the Holy Ghost. Teaching them to observe all things whatsoever I have commanded you: and lo, I am with you always, even unto the end of the world. Amen. This segment of scripture written by Matthew gives us clear and concise evidence that the work of the church is not in the four walls of the church but in the field that is considered the world. The church serves as an incubator or a hospice for sick to be healed and those lost to be found. In other words, the church is a training ground for development in servitude that will reveal purpose and destiny.

The Church has ever been a depot for pimps, prostitutes or players to undermine the integrity of God service for the kingdom.. There are men of God who like to gather grapes (gifts or gifted men or women) so that they can extract their gifting for personal gain. These men may have preached out or birthed many churches but have nothing to show for it. In other words, they think that it is their job to come to a perfect stranger to lure them under their covering. There are some that God has made with genuine hearts of a father. While there are multitudes of men who feel that covering is unscriptural, they will attempt to figure out that God had already spoke it out. Whenever there are genuine fathers who are more concerned with development of their Spiritual Children than how much money they can receive. Some of these culprits feel that they have more to offer you because they have a building and a whole lot a debt.

More often than not, these leaders are only out to suck them dry so they can claim the number of churches under their covering. They have people in the building but don't require any standard of living. If you look at their home, you will see it jacked up to the point that the kids don't even want to attend church. This is clear evidence that the kids have an open view of how their parents act at home. Many of the children run from the church because they see the true lifestyle their parents portray in the public and at home. There is a vicious intent to deceive the body of Christ in their intent to lead others outside of their fold. The cosmetic view of this type of leader is always caught up with promiscuous affairs with women at the local church and those in their extended covering at large.

This type of toxic leadership is atypical when the wife is silent only to protect the public view of her husband. This is the classical type of leaders that is always at his member's house and in some cases without any accountability gets in trouble with the husband. Some leaders think that it is ok to be in members home or a friend's home without the husband at home. The bible tells us in Romans 14:16 "Let not your good be evil spoken of." So many leaders think it is appropriate to be in the house of single women without any level of accountability. It has come a time where you can not be in your office without some level of accountability. The problem of promiscuity among male and female that a leader must be careful to always have accountability.

There are cases where woman and men are sent in as culprit to set their leader up. In this case, they ask for a counseling session with their leaders and then make sexual advances. In this case, the leader rejects their advances and the culprit stand up and start screaming while ripping their own clothes off. In the same breath, they are shouting stop, stop don't touch me and running out of the office. This is tactic used by some women to draw attention from other members who rush to her distress call. Furthermore, the distress call is more damaging to the leader merely because those members who run to the scene are pawns in the victims plot. The leader has placed himself open without any accountability to defend himself. Unfortunately, these leaders try to rely on a perceived trust of members in a delicate scenario. In a lot of cases, it is a setup but this whole scenario would be null and void if there were others in the closed door conference session to see their current posture. In effort to defend himself, the Church Leader has been made to look as the attacker when he or she has not done anything.

If the Senior leader would assembly a staff to serve as Lay Elders, Armourbearer's or Adjuvants, this would give them a protective shield when counseling with members. The employment of applications as mentioned above would also give its leadership wise counsel and structure for accountability purposes to leadership who visit member's household. No one would be able to use this tactic that the enemy has employed to be an accuser of the brethren.   Unfortunately, this counter action also hurts leaders who entertain promiscuous behaviors in sleeping with their Spiritual   Children.   The   incest   is   further compromised by giving them money to keep quiet and a promise for a position in the Church.

Some of the women are not members   but pretenders sent by the devil to seduce leadership who promise to leave their wives. Alarming reports have surfaced that indicate that some Leaders, both male and female, are inundated with affairs with many partners inside and outside the Church. Some Church leaders engage in activities in brothels, drug houses and gambling establishments. The bible says in 2 Timothy 4:3-4, "For the time will come when they will not endure sound doctrine, but after their own lust shall they heap to themselves teachers, having itching ears; and they shall turn away their ears from truth, and shall be turned unto fables." There are many cases in America where the servant leader begins the process of counseling and the counseling session ends up in the bed room with the one they are counseling candidates. Some these men serve as pimps, players and prognosticators of sin.

The spiritual leprosy is a violation of Gods ordinances and it is reproach against Gods design for relationship in matrimony. These individuals only entered into ministry to lure women into the bed of and build a since of loyalty to their leader and not to the God of the leader. The tables have also turned because woman are currently heads of churches and they are luring young men into their beds. In essence, this is not just about men or women, but about the carelessness of sin(adultery and fornication). There is a new demonic premise infiltrated in the church that some men teach and convey that sex with another outside of your marriage is profitable. Some these men dislike their wives so much that they are with only their mate for public image purposes. Furthermore, this spurious mirage of an image is only for the pretense of public concession. In a nutshell, the marriage is only a mirage to make their public image appear to be substantiated.

The façade presents an appearance of a strong marriage when in essence it is a marriage of convenience. The spirit of divination comes with leaders who their spiritual daughters to follow their husbands in the faith. However, the enemy has invaded and instruct their daughters to strong arm the mates come to their church. This strategy would be great if this person lived in another town and the lord was sending him to the area that she resided. However, this type of leader is controlling, domineering and manipulating daredevil. In other words, this leaders feels he has invested too much into her. He is upset that he has invested so much into her for him to lose his investment. This leader has developed a soul tie with her that is ungodly and may have encountered sexual relations. Men like this like to hold on those disguised as daughters but he has been having sexual relations with her.

Moreover, this man does not want her to leave because he gets zero return on his investment. Furthermore, he will not give his blessing because they will not be a part of his church. Some Leaders instructs their daughters to inform their prospective mates that they will not marry them unless they join their spiritual fathers church. True followers of Christ will seek out the spiritual father to seek and secure the Patristic blessing. The Patristic Blessing is a rites of passage that they covey to the couple intending to enter into matrimony. This is purely manipulation and control for men of God to use their own personal inhibitions as a spiritual father to make them choose between the spiritual father or her prospective husband. This is a selfish man to act out when a daughter seeks happiness for her rib cage and the leaders chooses to be bitter because she is led to go with her husband.

This type of church leader is so selfish because he feels that she should have told her perspective husband that she would only marry him if he becomes a part of her church. Now, this approach surely gives a great enlightenment as an true indication of how some leaders develop such unholy alliance with their spiritual daughters that they don't want to release. Some of these leaders have crossed the lines with their daughters by stepping into forbidden territory of adultery. This is supposedly classified as a mistake that should never have happened. This is also a trap that has happened with those who work so close together. Unfortunately, these men have become so dependent on their value to the ministry or church that they cannot exist without their co-dependency. The purpose of sons and daughters are to discover, disciple and deploy.

Every person that comes in the doors of the church should be developed to serve in the church through gift assessment. There should be more than one person handling the business aspect of the church so that if one is away the other is available. This strategy will enable to the church to exist and empower to equip others to serve in a variety of positions. Many marriages have been hindered because the set man has been more focused on a building than he has his own family. These men have exhausted their efforts to build the church and the family has suffered at the hands of a man who does not understand divine order. While this may be the cause in some churches, it is most assuredly not the case in all churches. Some men have learned to balance the equation to have a healthy relationship with Christ, his wife and children and the church. On the other hand, there have been many that have lost their families due to neglect and disrespect. The problem is that so many men view the church as the kingdom. Even though the church is a by-product of the kingdom, it is most assuredly not the kingdom in its self. Moreover, it is important to make note that the work of the kingdom is not in the four walls of the church and definitely not indicative of a message of three points and a poem. The blatant disrespect from some of the most bias people in the world are sitting behind four walls. They figure that you must be inside the four walls of a denomination in order to do a true kingdom assignment. While they are also very critical of your task and approach, they will always have an excuse why you should be at their church. How can you continue to fellowship with people that don't have the same belief system. While some say they use a piece of fish as a model to eat the word of God, there is always some dark meat and some white meat.

In other words, you may eat some dark meat and not like it but it may be good for you. Some leaders have switched from the position of evangelist to become a Pastor. However, an evangelist will never be an effective pastor because he carries the mark of the evangelist. The difference that most don't realize is the one can carry an evangelistic anointing and not be called as an evangelist. Part of the mark of an evangelist is a strong quest for souls to be won into the kingdom. The same sentiments can be said about the other functions in the five fold. Competition and jealousy are two of the biggest deterrents in the Church. The seed of discord is sown in effort to sway one member from another. Even some go to the extent to try lure the wife of one leader from her church in order to get them into their church. This has become another problem with fellowship with people who only desire is to steal sheep. They not only portray a notion that they only preach the word of God, but the truth of the matter is that they also desire to pack their church with other churches members.

This is not the case with leaders who have strong relationship with their members and don't look to lure with gimmicks that some folks use to get money. One of the biggest problems is that you can a mega church full of people but they don't take care of the church because they are not tither's nor givers. We have clearly missed the boat and some cases we don't even acknowledge an adequate portrayal of the word. One of the most abused scriptures is always quoted with poor understanding. According to Matthew 11:12 the bible says, "And from the days of John the Baptist until now the kingdom of heaven suffereth violence and the violent take it by force."

The only reason the believers do not fully understand their authority is that their leaders does not understand how to teach them that they need to get in the word for themselves to understand their authority and job description. In other words, the kingdom suffereth because the inhabitants of the kingdom have given the enemy the access code to come in a take it from them. In some cases, the enemy did not take it from them. The inhabitants of the kingdom fell asleep and allowed the enemy to walk in with no struggle. When God plants leaders inside of His Church, it is his responsibility to prepare and train them to maintain their post. It is the sluggard mentality for them to abandon their responsibility and allow their post to be unattended. In another sense, it is caused by leadership that is afraid to prepared saints for their assignments and delegate authority to those faithful to the vision of the house.

Consequently, there is an old system where the people are afraid to move without being castrated by this old style tyrant of leader. He blames everyone but himself and it is only his fault because he has limited his understanding of leadership and he thinks that he can use control or manipulation to scare them into his way of doing things. This is the type of leader that will tell you to get out of his church. This type of leader forgets that it started with God and is completed with God. The people under his care and control are limited in what they can do and often told what they cannot do. Instead of being seen, he should be un-noticeable, unstoppable, unseen and unpopular. There are too many men that desire the praise of people and do not desire to be stand for the truth. Luciferian's are nothing more than a satanic group of seekers that desire gods glory. These creatures of darkness have promulgated a stage for performance to see if they can trick believers out of their destiny.

The wolf in sheep clothing is the master plan to act like a believer with the intent to lead them astray. The devil can transform himself into the angel of light. This is how certain preachers have prepared their game plan extort from believers and make strides to foster their true agenda is to cause many believers to miss out on their destiny. The stage continues to be disseminated and the performers are continually working their craft of deception. Now this culprit is known by many for usury. If he or she cannot get you to do what they want for free or do it as a service to the church, they will label you as someone who is a selfish and a lover of money. In response to their efforts, they should realize that it cost to do ministry and those who are led to help will provide whatever seed the lord places on their hearts.

The efforts of some churches will try to make you feel obligated to give more to them because they represent the church. Whenever a church needs a speaker for a particular event, they only invite speakers who have a following or is good at raising money. This is clearly a church who is more concerned about exchanging money rather than getting a word for your church. So, it is a perception that a person with the word from the Lord cannot bring a blessing into their church. The leaders of this type of ministries come from a hidden agenda to invite churches out on mentality to only increase their effort to raise money. This beggar mentality is a facetious effort to thwart those desiring to help with worthy causes to feel compelled to do more. This leader will always us underhanded efforts to bring money under the table. It is this type of leader that brings shame to the kingdom in its effort to rape the kingdom. This type of leader is only interested in money but is not about souls.

CHAPTER 4
RIBOLOGY 101: EXPOSING THAT THE FALSE RIB

The ribcage of a man consist of twelve pairs of flexible, archlike ribs from the lateral portion of the thoractic cage. In the case of God taking one of the ribs to form a woman. It is clear that God had his hand in this entire process and created a woman that would compliment Adam. So, it is safe to say that Adam did not have to guess whether Eve was actually bone of his bone and flesh of his flesh. Adam & Eve was the mere foundation of creation and the first family that God had established. This was a sure thing that he had exactly the wife that God had in store for him.   Now, this is a great object to literally have God take a rib out of your body and present you with the wife of thy dreams. If everyone had this type of experience with God in their mates being presented to them, the divorce rates would not be in the predicament that they are in.

According to Proverbs 12:4, the bible says, "A virtuous woman is a crown to her husband: but she that maketh ashamed is as rottenness in his bones." For the most part, many people have heard throughout our society about this virtuous woman. The bible expresses in Proverbs 31:10. "Who can find a virtuous woman? For her price is far above rubies."   In other words, God has given us a mandate to seek for the woman that is designed to fit into your age. Furthermore, there is another type of woman that presents herself as a candidate to become a wife. The bible gives and exodus clause in proverbs 6:5, "Deliver thyself as a roe from the hand of the hunter, and as a bird from the hand of the fowler." An odious wife is one of great curses of life. A bad wife is more bitter than death. The odious woman is characterized as a type of Jezebel. She is often overly aggressive and uses her position gained from an non-delegated authority. It appears deceptively that she honors her husband but this is a trick in an effort to demand authority and dishonor her head.

Ecclesiastes 7:26, "And I find more bitter than death the woman, whose heart is snares and nets and her hands as bands: whoso pleaseth God shall escape from her; but the sinner shall be taken by her." The bible has given us evidence of this woman is full of hatred, bitterness and jealousy. In other words, she does not honor her husband but she desires to destroy him. This destruction is premised because the doorway of competition has gained access. Compatibility is an extreme issue in marriages today because people have certain unrealistic expectations for their mate. Some women only desire to have a man for the sole purpose of paying their bills and for sex.

While this may be the case for some, it is most assuredly not the case for all women. There are some women who desire to have their soul mate and willing to submit in accordance with the bible. On the other hand, there are some who only want to get together because they desire all their problems to be resolved. It is mere foolishness to assume that just because two people got married there would be no problems. This concoction is purely mind blowing to see that there are people who think and believe that the wedding ceremony will solve all their problems. Too much chagrin, this is where they need to have a reality check. In these cases, each rib offered a different perspective and required different needs. In the first case, rib number one was a much older woman that presented herself as an extremely confident individual, full of the Holy Ghost and committed to her husband.

However, this was not the case because this rib did not understand the need to leave and cleave. In addition, this rib was not properly prepared to do the basic task of cooking. On one occasion rib one cooked some fish, her husband sat to the dinner table and attempted to use a knife to cut a piece of the fish. It was a futile attempt and a unsuccessful endeavor because the fish was overcooked. This rib thought that it was ok to travel every week to spend time with her mother, come home on the weekend prepare some pre-meals for the entire week and go back to her mother's house. Marriage is a union between husband and wife. How can you bond with someone who desires to spent most of her time with her mother in a city approximately 100 miles in distance from our home. The extensive travels grew worse to the point that on one occasion, the first rib ask her husband to come down with her to spend the weekend with her mother. Because of the obscure living conditions, he asked his wife where in the world would they sleep and she informed me that she would be sleeping with her mother and informed him that he would be sleeping on the couch.

The husband informed his wife that under no circumstances would they be sleeping in separate beds. He informed his wife that he would not accept those arrangements. Further, he instructed her that he would drive her to her mother's house and allow you to bond with your mother as long as you desired. The husband told his wife that he would return home or stay in a hotel because he did not get married to sleep on a couch by himself. In other words, this rib spent more time at home with her mother than she spent time with her husband. Although this extended time was primarily due to a surgical process that gave her time off.

Instead of spending it with husband, she decided to run home to be with her mother. This rib was the type of woman that desire to be a stay at home wife and work on hobbies such as sewing and designing clothes. Due to the injury of her hand, her current job allowed her special medical leave despite the short time on the job. In an effort to get more time off, she called her job without discussing things with me to demand more time off. When the agency informed her that the doctors had sign off for her to return to work, she quit the job because she couldn't get more time off. This rib was self-destructive in her effort to manipulate her husband into allowing her mother to come and live with them. Part of my concern for my hesitancy, her mother and uncle were extremely heavy into witchcraft.

Early in courtship, she had shared that her mother attended church but had not totally been delivered from dabbling in witchcraft. To further the assertion, this rib instructed her husband not to eat nothing her mother would fix him. The mother in law of this rib always had a plate of food prepared for me whenever he came to visit. The first rib told me do not tell her that you don't want the food but to take it and throw it away once you reach the nearest garbage can. Within the next few months, his wife grew increasing homesick so she decided to go home. Because of her desire to be with her mother, he eventually severed ties through a divorce. After ten years of being divorced, the longing to find a rib was heavy on his heart. He had been living in the state of singleness in the state of North Carolina.

Through an encounter with a preacher, he introduced this brother to his sister and they began to dialogue over the phone for an extensive period of time. They planned to meet one another and the discourse began that would eventually lead them into marriage. On the surface of the relationship, it would appear that the two would be the ideal couple. However, there were some rare checks and blemishes that were highly recognizable. This second rib loved to pray but always had this hair dole on her head. This religious practice was not a belief in the intent to serve as a spiritual covering. He had seen this with one of his spiritual mothers back in the town he was born in. He was somewhat disturbed at the extent of her believe that God would not hear her prayers unless you had a hair dole on her head. After further consideration and my opposition to this form of commitment to the hair dole, he told her that he would not get married to anyone with these types of beliefs and/or conviction.

They parted ways for a brief moment and she called him and pledged her vow that she would not need to have a dol'e on her head. As a result they got married, and all hell broke loose. From the very beginning, there were some extreme issues with the family with an harsh history of bipolar and schizophrenia. This experience literally took the breath of me. It started with my mother in law who was and is severely diagnosed. The second rib has a serious relapse to where she was 8-9 years of age. In one sequence, she thought that he was her brother and she would give him instructions to go to the store to get some designated item. Furthermore, he would get calls from family members who knew that something was wrong. It was such a bizarre experience that one day he had to call the medic personnel to come to the house as a result of a schizophrenic outburst but they could not take here unless he had her committed. It was too early in the process and he did not have clear understanding about the nature of bipolar or schizophrenia. After diving in the research mode to find all that he could about the above mentioned subjects, he was better prepared with knowledge on how to handle any future encounters. One night he had an encounter with a demon that spoke to me.

The demon had convince this rib go back into a life prostitution from which she was delivered. He told me that he had to know power. He told that demon that his daddy had given him the power to bind and rebuke. He told him in the name of the Father through the Son Jesus Christ and the power of the holy spirit that he just received his eviction notice. God used her husband as an instrument to command the enemy to depart. Once the spirit of the harlot had left, He went back to her and closed the portal in order for the demon not to have access to return. This latter piece of the equation is often missed in deliverance meetings that will prevent the enemy from returning to the point where he was cast out. Rib three is a unique individual that he met in a church service meeting where an Apostle friend of his requested him to attend this service with him.

During the service, the Lord used this Apostle in such a magnificent way. Before leaving to return home, the lord prompted him to give the Senior Pastor a word. The Lord stated that he wanted her to set the house in order. He further instructed her that she was his prophet and not his pastor. Within her church, she had people in the wrong positions. The Senior Pastor broke down in tears and shared that she was aware of this but was afraid because of the location in which she lived. In her response she indicated that she wanted to make a lot of changes relative to the name of the Church and properly set this church up as God had directed. She asked if they could exchange numbers so that they could discuss this more.

This Leader had a delightful personality but she reminded me of rib 2. On the way home, the Apostle and a few other brothers were jesting with him about her. In return, he informed them that he was not looking for a wife. Needless to say, they ended up building a relationship that lead to marriage. In the first two months of being married, they were preparing to go to out of time for a preaching engagement. The door bell rang and there were three people and a big dog at the door trying to get in. It turned out to be rib three's son and his wife returning to the area with his best friend after being thrown out of the military.

Although he was grown and married, the abrupt return to home paralyzed their home with all the uneventful activities that would be going on. However, the son would brag about all the events that had occurred that they were never caught. However, he eventually was caught up in being at the wrong place and the wrong time. Eventually, he would be exonerated because of a mother's love. She was determined to prove their innocence. Finally he learned his lesson for that particular event. However, he had done so much dirt and never paid for those crimes. His mother could never see her child in a negative eye until they get arrested. The panic mode rises to the occasion and it is time where faith should be activated. Rib 3 was an educator, highly educated and extremely skilled in her own right as a preacher. However, she relied on the inspiration of other preachers who wrote books as oppose to the word of God.

The prevalence of some leaders to find so many underlings try to take an elite leaders perspective and then they look like a cartoon character when they fall. Needless to say, rib 3 tried to take over the church but failed miserably in her attempt. The damage was done and the relationship was extremely tainted because of her insecurity. Rib 3 was a classic case of a hurt individual that only hurt others with her disposition. As a leader, she was pretty God but as a follower, she was terrible. This rib is an individual who embrace truth on her terms but seldom stepped out to change the mindset of the people. Misrepresenting the truth was always her modis operandi. Lying to make herself look better than another. After all that was done and said, He gave this rib another chance and displayed to the true character of an odious wife.

This woman was so bitter because she the relationship to aim for a bigger platform. The husband had his own fault of loving a person who was likened to a damsel in distress. This relation was best characterized as a person looking for a platform that she did not have access and trying to take something from her husband that she never had before. With this rib, she operated in rebellion from the beginning and was sat down. Moreover, she could not embrace discipline so she returned to her grand fathers church who had just been installed by her auntie as the first woman pastor. Within two months of rejoining the family Church, her auntie licensed and ordained her on niece the same day. This is a classic case of King Jeroboam serving in leadership with the ability to qualify new leaders through intense preparation. The only problem in this matter is that this woman gave credentials to a woman with no training or equipping had taken place. To make things worse, the pastor became extremely sick and her untrained niece (rib 3) took over the church as the New Pastor.

This journey was a jagged one because she had so many people in her ear that prevented her from listening to God. It was quite clear that there had not been much training because she did not know how to council members without sharing personal matters with other members. The spirit of the sabotage awakened in her that she made a pack with the devil to attempt to destroy her husband's life. She was truly likened to the leviathan spirit which is a destroyer of ministries. This rib did not like order and simply did not have an understanding of the role of a woman as a wife. This woman epitomized the example of an odious woman. This woman could not follow and felt she could spend money out of the churches account without board approval.

The woman was a prophet, but she was doing the work of a pastor. Even though she was given instructions by her husband the bishop, she thought that she was above accountability. People began to see that the bishop and wife were not on the same page. Consequently, the marriage went into downward spiraling effect. This rib was the epitome of a odious woman. This woman never intended to know her husband. She only want to have access to his influence of friends. It was purely an attempt to enlarged her territory as she was looking to make a name for herself. She was not a part of the decision making board. After a series of events, the executive board shut down the ministry because and the rib and one of the members took a large sum of money out of the churches account. This particular rib followed her spouse to my current place of residence and landed job.

The rib moved to a new city and continued her divisive agenda. She literally thought that she could hinder him but she failed miserable. She even went through conspiracy like attempts to hinder her ex-spouses current marriage by bringing forth lies in effort to destroy the new relationship in his life. He was so elated when she informed him that she had been found by a new man. The ex-husband wanted the ending to be amicable because that is what they should have remained. All the heart ache would have been avoided and the discourse would not have been prolonged. Nevertheless the greatest blessing that could ever occur was the day I received my divorce decree in the mail. I am grateful for the freedom and to know that I don't have to go down this path any longer. I was determined not to be the covenant breaker. However, she did it only to marry another man and I am so happy of my liberation.

CHAPTER 5
AN EXPOSE OF BEING UNEQUALLY YOKED

When the Lord God created the institution of Marriage, he epitomize it by requiring that each person stand before God to be examined on the essential beliefs to make oneself compatible for marriage. Many people forsake this step because they are more eager to get married to solve another problem. For some, it is to move out of their parents home. For others, it is the desire to be independent. The motives could be endless but they end up being from an unrealistic standpoint. Many feel that a man or woman can make them happy and assume that happiness means the same thing to everyone. For some, they focus on security, money, cars, clothes, big houses etc.

The least of their concern should be involved with things rather than feelings of being in love between each other but to be on one accord with Jesus Christ. In other words, the power of agreement does not matter as long as she gets her way. When the motives are not pure, some women will use love as a wedge to manipulate their husband to get there way. Another problem that is often times forsaken, the subject of religion is side swiped when it comes to faith and how the children shall be raised. In the oasis of the marital development, the discussion was overlooked because the two were thinking in the now. Instead of looking into the future and planning for children development in Christianity, the two were only interested in the process of lovemaking. This is a problem in society because so many of church women and men have been waiting for this day. For those who have longed for this kind of intimacy in righteousness, there are firework's going on in the chamber room.

For those individuals who epitomized curiosity in the essence taken by those characteristics of embracing a inquiring minds mentality, there is this inward dialogue that says, "I know they had sex before they got married." Nevertheless, only the individuals know and God knows if the covenant they entered had been breached. One thing for sure, there is a spiritual impartation that will take place. Aside from the inquiring minds, there are those cheering on the side lines and some who are waiting to find out how was the chamber room experience. Some don't believe it is possible to wait and get married before engaging in the chamber room activity. The short lived experience is often a missing link when the parents get so intrinsically involved in the marriage and love making that they did not plan for an instantaneous pregnancy that sometimes can hinder the growth of the newly married couple.

It is important that each couple will spend quality time in getting to know one another and to plan the ideal time add children to their family structure. Although children are a blessing through the union of a husband and wife, it should be planned thoroughly so that the couple don't feel the children are a burden on their relationship. The children have now come and the honey moon is clearly over. Now, the family business should be centered on how to raise the children in terms of establishing a religious foundation. Neither one thought that it was import to have a discussion as to what faith they were going to raise their children. This is one of the problem areas when a household is established with two entirely different preferences of faith.

The world is always saying there is only one God, it should not make a difference. One the contrary, these details does make a difference. While the statement should be reiterated, there is only one true omnipotent and omnipresent God. All the others Gods are inferior to the one holy and infallible who is self appointed and self existent God. Sometimes, these choices affect their families in the spiritual arena. Because there is a lack of emphasis on the spiritual development in the body of Christ, most assume that they have it without any acuteness in being on the right frequency. Spiritual warfare is alive and the church definitely needs to be in tune with God. It should be noted that there are many voices speaking in the atmosphere but there is only one voice that carries all authority. The bible says in James 4:7 "Submit yourselves, then to God. Resist the devil and he will flee from you." James indicates that you must submit yourselves to God first and foremost.

Once this task is completed, then you are enabled to walk in Gods authority as a delegated ambassador, you can resist the devil. As a result of the devil honor for Gods authority, he will flee from those who work the word and walk in his spirit. Many have part of the equations perfected but lack the intangible to really walk in as a Spiritual Warrior. However, it is the latter part of walking in the spirit that is a missing ingredient. This spiritual enablement is available to all believers who trust and believe in the fullness of the word of God. Unfortunately, many professed believers attempt to read the bible just as if it's regular book of stories. The failure to comprehend the power in the word of God prohibits most believers from reaching their maximum potential. The old regime was to arrange marriages when it should have been to pray and seek God for the right relationships. In other words, there are relationships that were established on good principles and good intentions.

Keep in mind that good intentions are just a noted endeavor that is designed to help God when he needs no help from us. Marriages were designed to be the divine union between a man and a woman. The design & institution was patterned with the culmination of the body of Christ being betrothed. From an introspections standpoint, God does not have another option for a bride. The church in its purest form is the mode and model for us as we look into marriage. God has given us the opportunity to glean from him as he prepares for his wife. The bride of Satan does not have a chance reconnect because she has been earmarked for eternal damnation. Because of the human dimension of marriage, the spiritual intent was designed to be pure and needful for the true believers to understand its purpose and intent of the institution of marriage.

The main focus of marriage to the right person should be the uttermost criteria of epitomizes a model by design. Every person that stands before the lord for marriage, whether a believer or not, makes a vow to the lord for candidate that stands ready to enter into matrimony. The nagging notion of many people getting married under conditions that exacerbates being unequally yoked is so phenomenal. In a sense, they do not realize that just being married is enough to carry you over the mountain top. It is essential that nuances of marriage can be difficult especially sense everyone changes over time. The importance of pinpointing the complementary designed of God orchestrating the connection of a wholesome relationship minimizes the struggle.

The atrocity lies in the notion that many don't think that there are going to be some differences because two people are becoming one in the spirit. When the merging process did not take place (or should I say the incorporation process), there is a refusal to become one in the eyesight of God. Instead of being equally yoke, the unequally yoke creates a problem in the arena of oneness.   The two headed freak shows up and creates of monster because there is no balance in the house. The heads have not completed in the transformation and now you have two trying to compete with one another. This creates a downward spiraling affect in the family substructure and prevents a heavenly alliance to take its true posture.   In a true illustration, the person of a husband and wife are transformed to become the head and neck rather than two heads trying to walk as one. The misconception lies in the sentiments of people getting married for the wrong reasons to the wrong person. Many people would love to say they have a proverbs 31 woman as a wife.

However, some men have been deceived in selecting to marry an odious woman. The virtuous woman is designed truly to be a help meet. The bible says in Proverbs 19:13, "A foolish woman is clamorous(fool of noise): she is simple, and knoweth nothing." It is truly a time where the motives for marriage should not be for such things as security, money or prestige. These marriages are likened to time bombs waiting to blow up. On the other hand, some of these marriages will implode from the inside because there is no divine connection. It is essential that marriage is not treated like a meat market. Some make choices based of certain criteria that is either self-serving or subjective. Nevertheless, most people get married because they desire to be joined together by their divine mate as it is given from heaven.

Everyone desiring to be in the will of God should also have the same pursuit in their approach to their commitment to marriage. The shift had occurred from the stage from arranged marriages to ordained marriages. The seriousness of this endeavor is to present ourselves as a living epistle and serving as a model in the arena of marriage. Although many desire to get married, they don't realize that there is a permissive and perfect will of God. Getting married to the wrong person would be construed as Gods permissive will. On the contrary, getting married to the right person by divine will would be construed as the perfect will of God. Moreover, the choice is given to every believer to choose to make between the perfect will of God and the permissive will of man.

We must live with decisions that are made by human conscious and those aborted because we don't have an intimate relationship with God. Again, we face the dilemma of getting married based off a feeling instead of hearing the voice of God. Operating outside the spiritual arena, you can end up with the spouse from hell. As we look further in the matter of being unequally yoked, we must examine the reason for getting married. The number one reason for men is sex. The number one reason for women is security. Although both of the above mentioned reasons are valid in their perspective, it should not be the only reason. Normally, a marriage of a righteous man and righteous woman should be bound by a true relationship with Jesus Christ. When a person comes into a true understanding of the dynamics of real authentic love (agape, philia, storge, eros), a person can perhaps glean from and gain a better perspective of marriage. The bible says in Hosea 4:6, "My people are destroyed for lack of knowledge: because thou hast rejected knowledge, I will also reject thee, thou that shalt be no priest to me: seeing thou have forgotten the law of thy God, I will also forget thy children."

Rejecting God is truly an unwise jester because it will trickle down perpetually to the ensuing generations. The quest for understanding the nature of being unequally yoked is a timeless endeavor because of the wide spectrum of its meaning. However, most people view this subject matter from a very narrow perspective and it has caused some to be contrary to its true understanding of its ambiguous meaning. There is a much wider need for understanding in terms of being "unequally yoked." Perhaps, one could look at it in the most extreme manner of a Christian marrying a Muslim. The struggle would occur in how the family and children rearing in their religious beliefs.

The family attempts to give their children an opportunity to experience both side of the faith. This would be characterized as a house divided in the most essential areal of family development. Because of the continuous warfare to come on one accord, each member to decides to pray for answers. This creates a major problem because the dual deference to two different Gods. This is where many people insert the inundated notion that everyone serves the same God. This fraudulent concept has hood winked many to think that they can serve multiple Gods without any spiritual warfare. The divided house on one side is prayer to their god and the spouse is praying to their God. The premise here is that allegiance to which God should be the question. Wow, to say this is actually happening and people do not understand the spiritual plight. There is war going in the same house and the children are in the midst of a spiritual battle. The sad notion is that the parents have no clue. The bible says in Ezra 10:44, "All these had taken strange wives; and some of them had wives by whom they had children." This scripture indicates that when either parent is ungodly and one serves the true and living there is enough evidence the Christians shall not marry an ungodly mate.

Many think this is a solution to those who were married as unbelievers and then one of them get saved. This is not a doorway to get a divorce because one comes into the kingdom of

God. If anything, it is an opportunity for the saved spouse to witness to the unsaved spouse. The bible says in 2 Corinthians 6:14, "Be ye not unequally yoked together with unbelievers; for what fellowship hath righteousness with unrighteousness? And what communion hath light with darkness? Apostle Paul informs us that God has granted us a guideline in terms of marriage. He shares godly wisdom with the believer not to yoke together with an unbeliever.

This is a major atrocity because many Christians grow weary and begin to conjugate with unbelievers because they are tired of waiting for the one that God had created for them. The spirit of compromise comes to the forefront with many believers in terms of sex before marriage and sex with others outside of marriage. The use of contraceptives is a worldly method of endorsing sex for those who entertain more than one sexual partner. This method is not a full proof method of stopping unwarranted pregnancy or contracting a variety of unwarranted diseases. It is a joy to Satan because this unholy marriage has so many access points for him to enter. Being given access to through those doors of opportunity, Satan will take advantage of this portal and walk through with the intent to create havoc. Until the door of access has been permanently shut, the enemy will always invade and terrorize his enemy.

CHAPTER 6
DOES YOUR PRESENT RIB INTER-LOCK INTO YOUR RIB CAGE?

The rib cage is designed to facilitate barriers that surround the essential organs such as the heart and other organs of man. The barrier's in question are called the ribs of every man. In actuality, the rib is referred to as the wife of the husband who is referred to as the ribcage. The bible says in Genesis 2:21-23, "And God caused a deep sleep to fall upon Adam, and he slept: and he took one of his ribs, and closed up the flesh, instead thereof; And the rib which the Lord God had taken from man, made he a woman and brought her unto the man. And Adam said, this is now bone of my bones, and flesh of my flesh: she shall be called Woman, because she was taken out of Man."

However, the bible indicates that Adam took possession of this woman which indicated that she came from his bone and his flesh. In this case, God brought the woman that came from him so that he could name her. This provision here is an assimilation of the wife taking on the name of her husband. Instead of Adam naming her, she took on his name of the man she came from. In the Old Testament, the last name was never used. Because of the emphasis scripture implied that God brought the woman to the man, it is the writer's insertion that this may have been the origin where the last name of the man became the last name of his wife. Whereas Adam was given the authority to name her, it is the preponderance of the writer to infer that the revelations presented by God that the woman should take on his name. It is important to note here that many marriages were prearranged as a custom of the time. If we were to imply that God was a part of this process, we would be misleading the reader historically.

The hunt for truth should be every believers intent and missive. None-the-less, marriages were arranged solely for business purposes and consequently hindered the flow of what true marriage was all about. In some cases, the arranged weddings were incentive to an impending merger of a major business deal. This custom was practiced in part as a method for the parties to feel a closer connection with each one sacrificing one of the children in the union of marriage. The bond of marriage was in fact a sign of a seal through the marital covenant. This was one covenant that God designed without a breach. Although the marital covenant was serious bond in faith, it served as a viable tool to solidify the deal. When you imagine a person that has been selected for another without knowledge or awareness of her human and spiritual intervention, it becomes clear that this is a credence of a marriage of convenience.

The nature of marriage should never be used as on arrangement in a business deal. What is a help meet? A woman consumed with being an in her husband's space is not to be assumed that she shares the same call. Every time purpose is promulgated in a man's life, the devil sends a damsel in the man's life to use their past hurts to comfort them. This is a strategic plan by the devil to hook the man into the matters of the heart in order to manipulate or control their mate in effort to gain access to the platform in which he is granted. Now Kingdom Solomon manipulated each business deal to include a daughter as a peace offering in brokering many of his business deals. Although King Solomon epitomized this approach in his business dealings, this was not the Lords intent to swap daughters in business.

The stretching of the latitude is to help meet the entire families needs does not carry the intent of the father in defining this concept. The incumbents in this type of dealing don't have benefit of embracing the natural things the spiritual and natural tenets to use the elements of things such as love, attraction, common interest or a host of others things that would be construed for two people to be in love. However, this would be more like a rigid contract that is more like legal agreement that is made without the elements of love. The sacred nature of marriage should only be united in the sanctity of Gods divine connection The ribs of a man's rib rack or cage play a vital role in protecting a man's essential organs. One of the ribs is suppose to be so close to the man, where God has taken to form his wife. If the parents consent to arranging a marriage, it would not be in the same likeness of God doing it because the union was not granted by our creators hands.

In essence, the parents step in the role of God without having the ability to take the rib from the male and form a woman in the likeness of our creator and God. This is an interference with the plan and will of God. As with every season stanza, man has attempted to be God with no authority but that which has been delegated. In this sense, there was no delegation of authority to step in the role of creator. No custom or man-made plan should interfere with the consent of two people aligning when the design had not been considered a match. In other words, God in his creative authority designed us by blue print. When the output does not conform to the designer's intent by design, there is a skewed reaction or malfunction in the process. No two people had the same design. Even to the point of twins, there is always a slight difference between identical and fraternal. People are fascinated with the idea of twins but are not necessarily educated about them.

Though the identical in physical features (usually one will be right handed and the other left handed) to the eye, one might be taller than the other or one could be shade lighter than the other. There are other factors that may cause one to consider an abstract notion in understanding the perplexity of twins. In the case of a set of twins getting married, there is a serious dilemma in determining which twin fits into the rib cage. If you place both rib's in the socket of the ribcage, you would be able to determine which one would lock in place. If the arrangement scenario was used, we could see the difficulties that could occur with the twins.

Because of the loose nature of marriage arrangement, this is a high probability in someone getting married to another that just does not fit. In a nutshell, the play indicated that this rib may not fit exactly as the other twin rib may have been the perfect fit. Even though the twins were identical, the opposite twin was a better fit for this particular rib cage. There is a famous play writer who depicted a serious where a husband has left for another woman. The wife of this wealthy businessman could not have children for some reason and her husband decided to work away from home. The deception had not just began at that particular moment because it had been going on for some time. So, after he won a prestigious award, he dropped her off to this huge house and told her not to wait up. Instead of spending time with his wife, he made plans to be with another woman who he had also shared her bed and the birth of their children.

He returned home to inform his wife that he wanted a divorce so he could give his children a home and rites of inheritance. Even though he had violated his marital covenant, he thought that he was getting a better deal because his current wife was barren. He felt that his business success would enable him as a celebrated business man.   Furthermore, he turned his nose down on his wife and threatened her with harm. This kind of man was heartless, arrogant and pompous. He forgot where he came from and did not realize what he had to until he was on the low end of podium of life. The woman that carried his children to term took them and his money and ran. This woman did not care enough to nurse him back to health. When the tables are turned and he was injured, his wife came back to nurse him back to health. This woman had been denigrated by her husband who in the face of serious health adversity needed her to do her wifely duties.

The woman he thought was there to love him was nowhere to be found. This scenario is just a overabundance of examples of women who desire to be treated like royalty but not ready for the real test of a crisis in the relationship. It is so apparent with women who are high maintenance fail to understand the importance of respect for the one that has been taking care of the bills. Instead, they do not want the responsibilities of a man that may or may not recover from a crisis. This type of woman is nothing more than a gold diggers that simply don't want to deal with any kind of adversity or responsibility. This other woman was only there to spend the money and live a life of luxury. This man trusted in a woman that he intended to marry but she bailed on him in a crucial moment in his life.

However, the woman that he disrespected took her marital vows seriously. In spite of the abusive behavior & betrayal, she returned to the aide of her husband to aide him in recovery. While the divorce decree was in the works, this woman has to make decisions concerning surgery that was a matter of life and death. On the other hand, the woman he intended to marry thought she had rights because she was shacking with him. The doctors could not act on the girl friends request because the wife was still legally married to him.   The wife made the decision to have the surgery and nursed him back to health. Although she was angry with him for the way he had mistreated her, she forgave him by putting aside the angry feelings and put his health as top priority. Needless to say, he recovered enough to realize that he made a big mistake.   They even started to attend church where he gave his life to Christ. During this phase of life and recovery, he realized that he had a rare jewel of a wife.

However, it was too late because had met the man that was really the rib cage she was designed for to be connected. Because life is full of choices, it is vitally important to make the right choice.   Some decisions are made foolishly with outside influences that can be destructive to the marriage. It is a foolish person that makes a decision based on natural intangibles without realizing the spiritual implications. The institution of marriage is a journey that is not cake walk but it will have trials and tribulations.   The enemy will tell you to get out of this relationship because there are so many fish available in the sea. However, there is a notion to eradicate someone quickly from the marriage because of inadequacies in their body composition.

The abdication of elements in a person's body does not give us the right to abandon the marriage. The vows taken in the marriage ceremony are taken seriously by God. The problem in society is that we make vows but don't take them seriously. It is a non committal society that has been brewing sense the eons of time. Whether it is the inability to have children or some other debilitating disease, the term divorce should not be considered as part in the equation. Love is much more abounding as we place Jesus Christ in the center of the relationship. Furthermore, the foundation of marriage is Jesus Christ. If he is not the center, the marriage will be shallow and doomed by powers of darkness. It is essential and a certainty that getting married is more than money, cars and houses. The bible is clear in its depiction that as surely as there is some peaks in life and some valley of the believers as well.

According the Psalms 23:1-6, "The Lord is my shepherd: I shall not want. He maketh me to lie down in green pastures: he leadeth me beside a still waters. He restoreth my soul: he leadeth me in the paths of righteousness for his name's sake. Yea though I walk through the valley of the shadow of death, I will fear no evil for thou art with me; thy rod and thy staff shall comfort me. Thou prepares a table before me in the presence of mine enemies: thou anointest my head with oil, my cup runneth over. Surely goodness and mercy shall follow me all the days of my life: and I will dwell in the house of the Lord forever" The devil tricked the man in the above mentioned scenario to think that someone outside of his marriage could provide him with the things he should have sought from God in the woman he had married. He allowed a demon to tell him that the affair he was having justified his actions because she could not conceive a child. This particular man chose to ignore one of God's commandment not to commit adultery. The spirit of adultery is so prevalent that it has invaded the world and the Church. The defiling of the sanctuary is more than just sex between a married person or non married person. The latitude of adultery had expanded into the Church to include manipulation with Spiritual parents and Spiritual Children as idols. This is an unfortunate endeavor and nuance of God for man to become an idol to those he has entrusted to be caretakers of his flock. In this case, the spiritual father or Spiritual mother had become a type of idol to them that the devil used with pride to defile themselves. They have compromised their kingdom values and brought this demonic behavior into the sanctuary of God. In most cases, they become slaves to those who are manipulators of their children to be pawns to get what they desire. In this case, the individual had forsaken their wife because of her inability to have children.

He abdicated from a God given covenant to secure a temporary feeling where love was not even the motive. He was manipulated and seduced by the spirit of the adultery. Now the same thing could have happened to the man. There are times when a man becomes unable to maintain an erection due to changes in their body from age or medical reason. This is not valid reason for a woman to commit adultery because of these uncontrollable conditions. This particular person had committed whoredom with a woman and shared the birth of some children. Needless to say, another man had come into the picture while she was a victim of this ultimate dejection and her heart was turned towards the other man.

The essence of this analogy is don't mistreat your rib because if you do, someone may be standing by on the sideline to pick your dejected rib and place it in their rib rack. This is a course of action where a divorce decree will be secured. Moreover, the negligence of this man showed that he thought he had an imperfect rib but he had forsaken her and allowed her to find a rib cage that would love her in the most intimate manner. In this case, the husband compromised and allowed her the unprecedented freedom to seek the opportunity to become a rib to another rib cage. Sometimes, it may appear to be construed as the wrong rib for one man and the right rib for another man. Because of his breach of the marital covenant, this man allowed her the opportunity to be found by another rib cage that she fitted in a manner that the click had already been established. This marriage was an example where the husband devalued her for things that she could not control but later found out that he lost woman that he learned that her value far exceeded in what he had perceived. However, it was too late because she had been found by a rib cage that only desire to connect with the rib of destiny.

CHAPTER 7
RIBCAGE DEFORMITY:WHEN A SAVED WOMAN SETTLES FOR THE TOXIC UNSAVED MAN?

Life is full of unsettling peaks and valleys that impact our society in such a profound manner. The pinnacles of life brings uneventful circumstances that condition's our mindsets in ways that does not allow us to prosper. Our prisons are of full of men and women the made bad decisions. Because of this negative pattern of living, many lives have been deterred due to this proactive reaction. The problem is centered through the notion that many people have been hindered because there is a poor pool of candidates for marriage. The nativity of this proclivity is that a poor pool of men is better than no man at all. Consequently, the supply brings a shortage of potential candidates. Therefore, the rat race for women to get married is placed on a time clock.

For fear of not having a mate, there are some women that feel that they must be married because all of their friends are married. The riveting notion is that there are women who rather have a shared experience rather than none at all. In other word, there is a repudiated notion that some folk would rather have a piece of a man than not have one at all. This pattern of stinking thinking carries a strong delusion for some women to feel a need to exercise a spirit of warfare in competition has come forth. Furthermore, the spirit of loneliness has set in and it fuels a desire for the flesh to be appeased. The spiritual struggles among even the faithful of believers have abdicated from the standard of righteousness. Several key male figures in Christendom have fallen prey to this cycle of events that seem to reoccur from time to time. The nature of this problem can be monumental in & outside the church.

The building up of your faith in your temple is a requirement to do your kingdom assignments. However, each member of the body of Christ must be able to live holy before they can demonstrate the essence of righteousness. The bible says in I Corinthian 9:16 "they that preach the Gospel must live of the Gospel." This verse does not imply financial appropriation only but it does require them to live righteously. The current trend of preachers being prepared for the work lives a lifestyle on a user friendly basis. Therefore, the social media plays a vital role in church marketing efforts to win the lost. The current trend of church growth strategy have lowered the standards of righteousness to win souls. The problem with this approach is that the social stream is a portal for pleasure. More preachers are spending time on the computers in these social media platforms entertaining others rather than spending quality time with their spouse and children.

Unfortunately, there are many spouses that use the social media as an effort to succumb to casual affairs. There are multitudes of women that released that they married a man that they really never fit. The signs were there in the very beginning but no one sought to deal with the issue at the time. They merely chalked it up to "the nobody is perfect" syndrome. Outside of the mere physical qualities, there is nothing that the two have in common. They bumped heads on everything and seldom agree on anything. This couple was doomed from the very start of the courtship. In spite of the signs, they overlooked them and decided to get married. This relationship had all the signs of a titanic eruption.

When the two overlooked some key ingredients regarding chemistry, interpersonal skills and the ability to communicate effectively with one another, they basically threw out the baby with the bath water.

This relationship is a typical relationship that is set to explode because each one had the same strengths and weakness. The scale of this relationship was not balanced and it would eventually tilt until the fall of destruction had occurred. This pattern can be traced back towards the prehistoric days when the best looking man and woman were put together. The ken and Barbie complex was established and it became the American dream. The massive marketing campaign to sell or purport the American dream has unleashed a deceptive image of marriage. It appears that many were sold on happiness by having the spouse, the Career and the stellar public image. In a sense, there is still an appeal to the dream to have someone that is smart, is articulate and is easy on the eyes. During the course of the relationship, the outer appearance has faded or withered away. This is a classic example of a shallow and prudent relationship.

It is apparent that the love was likened more to an empty callous. If anyone knows anything about a callous, they will find it to be hard on the surface and soft on the inside. When the hard surface had been peeled, you have access to inner portion of the scab. This image of marriage for appearance sake can be viewed in the likeness of a scab. The surface of the scab appears to be impenetrable which is what many would view most marriages built on this unsure and shallow foundation. Instead of realizing that there really is not a strong foundation, they rather live a lie than to accept the truth. As a result, many couples stay married but will embrace relationships outside the marriage.

The cosmetic marriage will take on a deceptive practice where the image is their but no real substance is present.   Unless you have experienced this process, you really won't be able to comprehend.   It is usually surrounded by a good idea that is most likely not a God idea. Although the mothers and older saints play cupid by seeing single individuals that they thought would make a good couple. So, they implemented and activated a covert plan get them together by any means necessary. The ultimate part of the plan was to get those young couple married. It should not be surprised or should it be condemned that these precious individuals tried to help God out in match making.   Unfortunately, every good idea is not a God idea. These precious individuals only mistake is that they failed to consult God in their efforts to unite the young couple. In this endeavor, we find that the mothers of the church were major supporters of marriage.

In other words, the two individuals got married and now they have to pay an enormous price because of the spirit of lust and loneliness. The propensity to revisit the past is a major just followed scripture to the letter but had a previous sexual relationship before committing to Jesus Christ. The mentalityof some Christians is with regard to sex outside of marriage is mind blowing. Furthermore, there are so many people with soul ties with former lovers and make efforts to rekindle the flame under the banner of righteousness. Why would someone desire to go backward in a time when they serve a God who is progressive in nature. The power of the forward thrust is enabled by the power of the Holy Spirit. It is an extreme necessity for the church to understand that there is no power in religion. A religious spirit would inform a candidate that God does not require you to be married to have sex. The major emphasis of the argument stems from the days of King Solomon, who was known for his wisdom and 700 wives and trend concubines.

Aside from the wives, King Solomon had access to 300 concubines for his good pleasure. God knows your strengths and weakness. He tells us furthermore, that God is love and it is all right for homosexuals to express their love. This kind of foolish speaking has nothing to do with God. It is derived purely from the devil for the sole purpose of contaminating the institution of marriage. The agenda has expanded to redefine the biblical definition of marriage as a male and female to include couples of the same sex. While it is true that God is love, let us not get it twisted that love of can be redefined for the sake of the homosexual agenda. Many untold stories have been revealed regarding some good marriages that have endured major hardships.

Some have just made the most of a not so good situation. It is extremely important to be married to someone that you fit. While homosexuality does not fit into Gods plan, there is a demonic agenda fueled to establish its own agenda. As we revisit the notion of shortage of men, some women feel that the homosexual agenda also is designed to prevent them from getting the divine husbands. It is not satisfactory to get a husband, but there is a mandate for those whom God Joined together to be united in holy matrimony. These current agenda does not want the traditional definition of marriage to be substantiated. The effort of society seems to be sedated when it comes to matters of sexual identity. It appears that many are in a drug like catatonic mindset. Furthermore, it gives that old impression when the television station went off the air and the static was continuously playing without anything on the air.

The value of life has dissipated to the point that anything goes without any reference to the purpose of God. Although many underworld members did ungodly deed, they still honored God religiously in a sense to attend church or a funeral. This new stanza of life in a redefined fashion of sexuality is not tailor made to the tenets of the word of God.   It is a true view of the world to become deformed to the point that the eyes of God does not recognize the very creation in which he formed. Mankind has deviated from his blue print. As a result, the institution of marriage has suffered tremendously. The value system has been reshaped to conform to the world which does not want to commune with the God who created it. The utter nonsense of a selfishness of society is perplexing to desire to create its own path of destruction rather than conform to the path of righteousness which was created with them in mind. Why settle for the mediocre life as presented by the devil? It is purely amazing that so many people do not have a clue about their God given rites of passage.

Apparently, the mind of master creator of the universe was thoughtful and loving enough to set a plan and purpose for each of us. In accordance to Jeremiah 29:11, the prophet says, "For I know the thoughts that I think toward you, saith the Lord, thoughts of peace, and not of evil, to give you an expected end. The Lord spoke through prophet Jeremiah and conveyed rather convincingly that he has made some plans for us. The plans in which he speaks of from his thought process to the believer is not suppose to be evil but thoughts of peace with an expected end. It is safe to say that God did not create a plan that would bring danger upon his creation or his believers.

The tone of the words of the prophet is an endearment from a father who just does not desire for his children to be done wrong. It is clear that he wants his children to be profitable in a positive way. For a Godly woman to marry an unsaved husband, this would definitely not be the will of God. It would demoralize the goodness that he has placed in them. Furthermore, it would pervert the good nature and intentions that God has in store for his children. If Gods thoughts are pure and good, then God would not want his daughter to be with a man that could not possibly treat them the way he has expected them to be treated.   The fact that she settled for an unsaved man is nothing short of ditch she fell in and got up with something that she found in the ditch.   The   imbalance   in   the   relationship furthermore purports that their spiritual walk will deal in more warfare because you have one serving the God of truth and the other following the God of error.   The nature of good and evil is combative in its discourse of existence. The fuel continues to intensify as the battle continues to progress until that moment when God says it is finished. The game of life is over and Jesus Christ is Lord. The victory is ours and we no longer have to settle for mediocrity.

CHAPTER 8
BITTEN BY SEDUCTION

The nature of a snake has forever been a thorn in the side of mankind. As far back as the Garden of Eden, the sly cunning nature of a snake had a lingering impact on society. The depiction of a snake is almost never positive because of the role it has played in society. Many people attempt to tame snakes in order to become pets but fail to realize that sooner or later the one attempting to tame will feel the affect's of a snake bite. Needless to say, there has been an increasingly new portal opening in the institution of marriage. Fornication and Adultery are major deterrents in the institution of marriage. his pattern is continuously increasing in size to further the crack and widened the gap of disparity. The premise of a snake is to walk in your life as a friend with the intent to get close to you. However, there is a preconceived notion that he or she wants what the other possess.

The nature of trust has abdicated in the institution of marriage. God is not pleased with these assiduous notions where no one seems to trust one another. This spirit has invaded the church and crept into various aspects of marriage. This is detrimental to the plight, purpose and plan of God. Marriage was designed to enhance each other's life. Because of the demise of so many marriages, it is a necessity that these trust issues be made aware and destroyed. This is a criteria that should be a mandate that couples trust ye one another. Without trust, it is a very difficult process in building a firm foundation. Because of the sinister nature of infidelity, many marriages are literally destroyed or hanging on the jagged edge of life. Why do men or women cheat? The answer to this question could literally change the venue of marriage.

Some men feel that they are not cheating because they love their wives and participate in an occasional affair that means nothing to them. Once the mindset of this thinking process was generated by those labeled worldly but, we have found this spirit has invaded the church at an alarming rate. Preachers have decided to be single but they engage in affairs with single or marriage women struggling with divorce. However, these same men would have a fit if their wives were to engage in the same game. What does God say about this pattern of behavior? How do preachers respond to their call to repentance? How should the flock respond when their leader is caught in a web of deception? How is this mockery viewed in today's modern world when a leader is found to be living a different life than the one he or she preaches about? More importantly, there should be a greater concern as to answering to God for such a behavior.

It is apparent that the very ones that piously declare that they love God have been found to be hypocrites. The enemy loves to invade this plateau with leaders because of their self assured attitude that this could never happen to them. As we look more seriously at this pattern, we can see that more leaders have developed a complex that implies there is no need to repent for their public indiscretions. This attitude has further invaded in the church and many are fearful that it may even have a detrimental impact on the current as well as future members of the church. While it is a true statement that spirits can be imparted, the church has no clue about the spiritual arena and its dimension.

The subtle nature of snake attempts to act like they are your best friends just to get close to you in order to squeeze life out of you. They carry the same sentiments of on a python. The primary scope is to befriend each person for the sole purpose of bringing division. Instead of giving sound biblical guidance, they will give you their own person empirical experiences. They will get you to close to you in order to bring a division between you and your spouse. They always have a word for you and will tell you that they see the spirit of your wife. The same tactic is worked in the women's arena is to constantly imply that they see the spirit in your husband. Some clergy will warn you to get rid of your spouse and others will go to them and tell them the same thing. This person is pretentious in their effort to be unbias. However, they never considered to enter in prayer to petition the Lord concerning this matter. This is a dangerous person because they focus on human intuition instead of tapping into the will of God.

They never should have been emotionally attached to this matter. This person allowed his personal opinions instead of trusting in the word of God. The serpent is clever because he or she purports that they are your only friends. In a nutshell, you will see that these type of friends don't have many friends.   At best, they have a lot of associates. The reason for this behavior is that he or she is worn out from working because he has nothing to show for his or her life.   In other words, this type of snake will work both sides and make one think he or she is your friend. While he or she know that you and your mate are dynamite together, he or she wants access to what you have but he or she cannot afford to pay you for your knowledge. This person is a user seeking glory for everything he or she has done. Life is spent by many seeking validation from people to imply that you would not progress unless you were somehow connected to them. This type of snake is only out for themselves seeking validation to make them look good.

Life has a way of revealing the heart of man. This person can never sit back and do his assignment without complaining. Instead of him working with what he has, he is ungrateful to have some people to listen to him. He is not satisfied because the people he has are broke, busted and disgusted in him. This person is always disgusted with the people that serve him because they do not have it like to other elite preachers. The problem with preachers like this is that they assume that because they have been doing this for 30-40 years, that they have been doing this right. If you can yourself and leader, why are you still taking money under the table. Why can't you stay out of the beds of those single women you are trying to win in the name of the lord.

Yes, it is amazing that you can to teach the principles of the word of God but you cannot live them yourselves. It is condescending for a preacher to preach to you about living holy and he is a victim of cant help it syndrome. This is why the church has not been affective because the leaders cannot keep their relationships professional and sacred. It appears that nothing in the church is sacred any longer. The bible says illustrates that the two sons of Eli, hophna and phinehas were engaging in sexual lude acts in the church. Eli was the father of these two children that God held in held accountable for their actions.   The bible says in I Samuel 2:12, "Now the Sons of Eli were the Sons of Beliel: they new not the lord." The word "Beliel" is defined of a person who chooses to serve the devil. The enemy is slick and sly in his efforts to gain entrance. If the devil can't get you, he will go after your children.

The devil will send people to act as friends but in reality they are a lot like a snake. This is the worst kind because they will use you to the uttermost and will not pay you a dime. The angle is centered around extracting everything they can get their hands in order to make them better than before. The agenda is about fame and self seeking glory that does not belong to you. Most people turn on the television and see those elite preachers who can afford the television cost. In their mind, they ponder at the notion of a hypocrite telling them to live one way and they are living another way.   The nature of competitiveness has invaded that church to bring more light to entertainment than it is about winning souls. It is amazing that more men and women of God are using Old Testament mishaps to justify their actions in this present day journey. It used to be a natural thing to be competitive in sporting events but now it has shifted to winning the race of being the largest church with a congregation of money exchangers. The fuel of church growth use to be about discovering a soul, disciplining a soul and deploying the soul into destiny.

The story of Joseph gives a discourse of a young boy who was favored highly by his father. His father Jacob favor him so much that he gave him a coat of many colors. This coat was designed and given a child that was the result of his wife of old age. Joseph was stripped of the coat of colors and place into a pit by his four brothers (Ruben, Judah, Simeon & Levi). They sold him to one of the officers of Pharaohs. While his brothers thought that selling him and stripping of his coat was a detriment to him, he was not stripped of his relationship with God. Joseph was now a slave in potifars camp and decided to make the best of it. He may have been banished from his father's house but he knew was not banished from his God.

Joseph established himself as a dedicated slave and soon was promoted by decree of his master making him steward of his household. This decree granted Joseph status and granted him access to his entire household. The historical precedence of Egyptian women was extremely promulgated as seducers of men. The plot had thickened as potifars wife approached Joseph to go to bed with her. Instead, Joseph honored his master house and his relations with God. Joseph refused the advances of potifar's wife to commit adultery and lived by the standards of righteousness that cultivated favor with him and God. However, potifars wife accused Joseph of rape to his master and her husband. It is purely a most shameful instance of impudence and immodesty of Potifars wife to approach a man for the purpose in enticement.

The shame of lust in which potifars wife desire to engage in sex with Joseph and a potential scandal of her efforts to have sex outside of her marriage. The nature of sin began in her eye gate as she gazed upon Joseph who was a Godly man and well favored. The story never gives the name of Potifars wife but the issue is she was daring and shameless in the sin of her heart. In actuality, the hand of the devil no doubt was in her actions to threaten Joseph to lie in bed with her or she would tell Potifars that he attempted to rape her. Potifar's wife was truly used as Tempter and Joseph was considered the bate in trap. The chastity in Joseph by the Grace of God, was enabled to resist and overcome this temptation. In all things considered, his escaped was a great instance of Gods divine power as he has saved others out of the traps set by the enemy.

This opportunity could have went the other way had Joseph been susceptible to her charm. Although Potifars wife was a beautiful women in the house, Joseph business led him to be in the house without any suspicion of being caught.

The fact that none of the family was in the house, there appeared to be no danger of them ever being discovered, or caught. Needless to say, Joseph was a man of God who walked in the presence of God. It is safe to say there are some real committed Christian that live a life of purity. If Joseph had any other convictions, he would have failed his test just like many others who could not say they were victorious in the Lord.

CHAPTER 9
WISE COUNSEL & WISDOM "HOW DO YOU KNOW WHO FITS THE CRITERIA"

Seeking wise counsel has become a major deterrent in the body of Christ. For fear of your misery being preached at the next church meeting, many have abandoned the efforts to seek and get counsel from Church Leadership. Nonetheless, there is a difference between spiritual guidance and counseling. In some circles, it is wisdom for pastors to articulate that they are giving guidance as oppose to spiritual counseling for fear of someone acting on the advice and the repercussion are the response of the information given by the church leader. Many laws suites have been filed and won as result because the church leader render counseling but are not licensed to do so.

Because of the serious nature of this matter, many churches have altered their verbiage to warrant the need when it comes to giving members counseling. The bible says in Proverbs 24:6, " For by wise counsel thou shalt make thy war; and in multitude of counselors there is safety." The writer is remised to share that you are in an ark of safety when you have men & women who can discern the same understanding of truth from the word of God. The empowerment of God ensues from a group of Godly people that will exercise his wisdom rather a group of isolated individuals that walk in worldly wisdom. According to the bible in Proverbs 24:7,"Wisdom is too high for a fool: he opened not his mouth in the gate." Kingdom Solomon illustrates that the standard or bar is too high for a fool to reach. While the nature of a human being is intrinsic in its core, there is a tendency to keep silent when you are in the gateway.

There are many people that know about the great wisdom that Kingdom Solomon displayed. However, there is a travesty in just knowing about it and experiencing it as well. The bible says in Proverbs 24:14,"So shall the knowledge of wisdom be unto they soul: when though hast found it, then there shall be a reward, and thy expectation shall not be cut off. The preponderance of establishing fear in church members occur when a leader tells the members that they a cursed if they leave the flock. This verbiage and initiative is a strategic effort to control members from seeking another church that might be more suited for them. It comes down to the 3M's phenomena. The 3Ms is characterized as Money, Members and Mission has been rendered as a more appropriate language for the service rendered to members of the church. The greatest disservice is that most pastors or church leaders are not fully aware the difference between counseling and spiritual guidance.

If a pastor claims to have credentials to say counseling, they better be able to back it up with certified licensing. The reason for this is that candidate could go out and using the advice and do something detrimental. This person could claim that he got the advice from his Pastor. The truth of the matter is the legal system could put the blame on the advice of the Pastor claiming that his advice lead his perishener to do the detrimental deed. The issue not could bring financial ruin to the church because the Pastor implied that he counseled the persons in which are now in trouble. The pastor cannot claim that the word in the bible gives him legal parameters to call it counseling. In other words, the Pastor could have made a claim that he gave his parishioner spiritual guidance.

The bible says in Proverbs 14:1-12, "Every wise woman buildeth her house: but the foolish plucked it down with her hands. He that walketh in his uprightness feareth the Lord: but he that is perverse in his ways despiseth him. In the mouth of the foolish is a rod of pride; but the lips of the wise shall preserve them. Where no oxen are, the crib is clean; but the lips of the wise shall preserve them. Where no oxen are, the crib is clean: but much increase is by the strength of the ox. A faithful witness will not lie: but a false witness will utter lies. A scorner seeketh wisdom, and findeth it not; but knowledge is easy unto him that understandeth. Go from the presence of a foolish man, when thou perceived not in him the lips of knowledge. The wisdom of the prudent is to understand his way: but the folly of fools is deceit. Fools make a mock at sin: but among the righteous there is favour. The heart knoweth his own bitterness; and a stranger doth not intermeddle with his joy.

The house of the wicked shall be overthrown: but the tabernacle of the upright shall flourish. There is a way which seemeth right unto man, but the end thereof are the ways of death. In a nutshell, Solomon has given us a summary of expectation of the role of a wife. A good wife is a great blessing to a family. Therefore, a fruitful wife has her family is multiplied and replenished with children that are built up in manners and refined in the ways of God. But a prudent wife, is one that is pious, industrious, savvy in business, and considerate, the affairs of the family are made to prosper, debts are paid, portions made, provision made, the children are well educated and maintained. The household is made as a home should be in the sense of comfort and creditworthy for a firm foundation. The wife is looked upon as the sustainer and maintainer of the household because the husband is noted as one who provides.

Many don't understand the true definitions of a husband because they see the work done by the wife as her doing but it is a delegated assignment by a good husband. The word husband could be parallel with the word farmer. It is also define as manager of resources. Many women take this notion that a man is weak because he gives his wife the money to handle the bills. However, he has delegated the responsibility to his wife to see that the bills are paid. This is not a trait of a weak man but it is a trait of a wise man. Part of the husbands makeup by design, he is the manager of the affairs of his house. The wife has been delegated responsibility to see that which was delegated by her husband is completed. While many will look at the current disposition of man, they will judge him due to his ability to read or write.

This responsibility does not abate the husband values but on the contrary, it substantiates his role as the head of the family. A foolish woman, on the other hand, has no fear of God nor any regard to the household business. She will only think of herself and her personal needs. This type of woman is willful and wasteful of resources through indulges her ease and appetite. In other words, this foolish woman placed her foolish appetite over that of her family. Thus, she will certainly ruin her household as if she plucked it down with her own hands. This woman is not wife material and needs much more preparation before she could ever become the proverbs 31 woman. As long as her heart has waxed cold, she has potential to become this mighty woman of God. However, some women will never become the "proverbs 31 woman" because they are cold, heartless and discredited.

The odious or contentious woman will only seek to marry so that she can destroy the man and take his possessions. In other words, this kind of woman would be a man's nightmare if he would meet and marry her. While it is true that wisdom begins with the responsibility of the mother and father, the family should also find themselves held to a high responsibility to the ways of righteousness. According to Proverbs 19:13-16, the bible says, "A foolish son is the calamity of his father: and the contentions of a wife are a continual dropping. Houses and riches are the inheritance of fathers and a prudent wife is from the lord. Slothfulness casteth into a deep sleep; and an idle soul shall suffer hunger. He that keepth the commandment keepeth his own soul; but he that despiseth his ways shall die." The writer, King Solomon, is comforted with the notion that a man can have temporal satisfaction in having a good wife and good children.

However, a foolish son can be a great affliction and could make any father wish that he was childless. A son that will apply himself to no study or business, will take no advice from anyone. Furthermore, he lives a lewd lifestyle and spends his money extravagantly or loosely in his current state of being. This type of son would bring grief to his father because he is a disgrace and is likely to be the ruin of the family resources and estate. Moreover, the father must choose to whom he must leave the fruit of his labor as an inheritance. A disrespectful wife is a great affliction to her household. Her contentions are continual every day, every hour and every moment to find occasion to make herself and everyone around her uneasy. This woman feeds perpetual vexation for her husband and leaves the house that shall not be repaired. The man under this madness has an uncomfortable life and has need of a great deal of wisdom and grace to enable him to bear his affliction and do his duty to scold his son and wife.

The distinction of every mans desire to have a discreet and virtuous wife is a choice gift of

Gods providence to a husband and wife that is prudent, which is in opposition to the one that is contentious. For a wife that is continually finding fault may this is wisdom or her personal resolution, it really is her lack of wisdom. Nevertheless, a prudent wife is meek and quiet and endeavors to make the best of everything. However, if a man has such a wife, let him not ascribe it to wisdom of his own choice or his own management.   But let him ascribe it to the goodness of God, who made him a help meet for him to be built up and not torn down. The bible says in Ephesians 5:22, 23, 24, 33, "Wives, submit yourselves unto to your own husbands, as unto the Lord. For the husband is the head of the wife, even as Christ is the head of the Church: and he is the savior of the body.

Therefore as the church is subject unto Christ, so let the wives be to their own husbands in everything. Nevertheless let everyone of you in particular so love his wife even as himself, and the wife see that she has reverenced her head. Happy and fruitfulness. Marriages are made in heaven. It is a true statement that a happy marriage is more valuable than houses and riches and the welfare of his family is attributed to Gods Favor. This good estate may be attributed by the inheritance of their fathers, which comes to course to a man. Parents that are worldly shall not comprehend because they are so busy disposing their children. The evils set in with men who are mindless of their own affairs as if they were cast into a deep sleep. Some spend countless hours dreaming of things but never implementing them. Some slothful people doze away their time, bury their talents, live a useless life, and are the unprofitable burdens of the earth.

The souls of some people are idle and lulled asleep. There are times when they appear to be awake but in essence they might as well be sleep. The state of perpetual sedateness is perpetuated by a say nothing or do nothing posture The abilities of some people that are in a frozen state or chilled because they choose not to use them. As they grow up to find that those who do not work cannot expect to eat, but must suffer hunger. An idle soul is one that is idle in the affairs of his soul and consequently shall perish for want of that which is necessary to the life and happiness of the soul. The happiness of the lord is towards those who walk circumspectly for those who make a conscience effort to keep the commandments of the lord in everything.

These are the ones to live by his rule and become servants of the King of kings and lord of lords. The perpetual misery shall exist for those who don't keep his commandments will experience a great deal of hurt and pain from their experience in hell. The choice to live according to their own ways, their own hearts, their chosen discourse of the world and never consider their destination, shall die and perish eternally in the fury flames of hell. The disconnection or connection to the Lord as the creator and sustainer of the souls created by him would be more productive for the world. Accord to Isaiah 55:8, the bible says, " My thoughts are not your thoughts, and my ways are not your ways, says the Lord." It is a pure atrocity that the world feels that they can embrace his ways without embracing him wholeheartedly.

Citizen of the United States do not fear God anymore. Therefore, the onslaught of these great atrocities of wrath shall come forth. According to Psalms 111:10, the bible says, "The fear of the Lord is the beginning of wisdom: a good understanding have all they that do his commandments: his grace endureth forever" Proverbs 9:10 "The fear of the lord is the beginning of wisdom, and knowledge of the Holy One is understanding" Proverbs 13:15 "Good understanding wins favor, but the way of the unfaithful is hard" Men or mankind can never begin to be wise until they begin to fear God; all true wisdom takes its rise from religion, and his its foundation in it. The principal of wisdom is to worship God and give honor to him as our Father and Creator. Those who have the holy fear and obedience to him. They understand that their obedience is graciously accepted as a plain indication of their mind that they do indeed fear God. A great understanding to those who have the knowledge of Gods commandments and can commit to learn them but a good understanding to them that walk according to them.

CHAPTER 10
FROM BEAUTY TO ASHES A MARITAL COVENANT ABRIDGED?

Throughout history, there has been a quest by men marry the prettiest girl or a quest by women to marry the most handsome man. It is through these times, we find that these surface items are always things that fade away. The inner beauty of a man or women should have a major impact on the heart of anyone desiring to be married. It should also be noted that the broad shoulders or biceps of man should not the only criteria for a women to get married. Neither should the only criteria for a man should be centered around any particular body parts of a woman. This is purely pathetic motive of those men the run their wives down after they have accrued a few pounds after birthing two or three children. In cases of the heart, men are too ashamed to be with their wives because their body composition has been altered. The sad case is that most of these men have gain more than 40 pounds of good home cooking and some of them spend a great deal of time drinking alcoholic beverages to aid in the added pounds.

Most practitioner's have no clue as to what a person is going to look like in 20 or 40 years from now. It is amazing how some that were beautiful from the outside in their youth and you will find that outer beauty of a flower faded away. In other words, it is a true indication that the glow of beauty can fade away in the natural but there is an inner beauty of holiness that will never fade away. On the other hand, there were those who were unattractive at youth that blossomed into someone very beautify and spectacular. According to Isaiah 40:8, the bible say, "The grass withers and the flowers fade but the word of our God shall stand forever." The writer's paints a picture of the grass and the flowers dissipate as with almost everything in life. However, he makes it clear that the word of God shall last forever.

The eternal father who is the eternal word shall last endlessly. It is purely amazing that life in the proper context has limits but the God of life is eternal. The lifespan of man is characterized by his purpose for his creator. In John 15:6, the bible says, "If a man abides in me, he is cast forth as a branch, and is withered; and men gathered them and cast them into the fire, and they are burned." The withering aspect of the above mentioned text implies that it will dissipate. The purpose and good pleasure of Gods creature is to serve him. If this creature does not fulfill its purpose he or she is cast into a fire. In other words, John is informing us that your usefulness to God is predicated on fulfilling the intent for which you were designed to do.

The enemy greatest tool is get the believer too deter from the intended purpose of the designer. If the enemy is successful, it give the designee a perception of the desire outcome a minus in its endeavor to achieve its created purpose. God has no need for anything that he has created when it does not accomplish his God given purpose. The common goal in this endeavor is too examine marriage and embrace the essence of covenant to bridge the gap in understanding. Because of the nature of premature marriages with no mandate from God, it is essential that each person should examine their lives before taking those vows.

Sometimes, God will instruct you not to get married because there is a need for both to be healed. In this case, God was not saying that they could not get married at all. He delayed the wedding because it was not the right timing at the present moment. God new that this marriage could not be prosperous without the need from healing to take place. Nevertheless, the two decided to disobey God and entered into a premature marriage. Deliverance had not taken its full course of action and the noncompliance of the dictates from the word that should have been headed. As a result of not allowing the healing to be manifested, the enemy had the combination code to walk in the front door.

With the access code, Satan comes in contact with fresh candidates that had good intentions to serve God fully but ended up serving the God of Darkness. The nature of darkness is precipitated in that light has been either turned off leaving the opportunity for those who are light bearers to bring an illumination of light into the atmosphere. The darkness is likened to the flesh of man in that it comes to strive or to appease itself. There is an eternal war with light and darkness that is identical to a fight with the flesh and spirit. Both of them are fighting to have dominion. Warfare is a natural phenomenon in both the world and the spiritual arena.

War is a combative platform where good and evil have engaged in a war to destroy one another. In the spiritual arena, the devil has been at odds with God since he tried to take over the realm of heaven. From the pavilion of Glory, God allowed a high ranking angel to attempt to over throw heaven because he had developed pride. Lucifer actually developed a mindset that he could do a better Job of running heaven than the creator himself. In a nutshell, he allowed his self absorbed pride to deceive him to think that he could out duel the very one who gave him the ability. This is an atrocity of a creature trying to out-think its creator in ability and mindset.

Keeping in mind that God is still anticipating the day of culmination, he can embrace his bride in holy matrimony. This is true model for the institution of marriage that God honors holistically. It is a natural tendency for humanity to look first on the flesh rather than the spiritual side. God had stated in the bible that it is first natural and spiritual. The bible says in 1 Corinthians 15:46, Apostle Paul says, " Howbeit that was not first which is spiritual, but that which is natural; and afterward that which is spiritual." It is apparent that God does the exact opposite of mankind. In other words, the God has given humanity a divine order to target the natural and then the spiritual. While the flesh is corruptible, the spirit man will be incorruptible and indestructible. Howbeit, when the two come together there is a divine quickening that causes a supernatural live giving experience as an inoculation by the Holy Spirit. This divine quickening of the Holy Spirit as it is interconnected with the human spirit of mankind.

This missing element is often confused with the Holy Spirit. There is an amazing grace to creation to be reconciled back to God since the days of the great fall that took place in the Garden of Eden. Every member born into this world has an opportunity to embrace the plan of salvation. Once they become believers through true conversion, they have been endowed with a point of access to the one who created them. Unlike prayers that have been petitioned to God without a connection being grounded, the grounding process comes when sinners covert through righteousness by accepting Jesus Christ as their lord and savior. There is a cosmic awakening in the pavilions of Glory when one soul is converted from the hands of the devil.

We must be reminded that God gets excited in souls converted into the kingdom because they become a part of his bride. The preeminence of this theory is that they get the opportunity to tap into their gifts and calling. In other words, each member of the bride is entitled to grow in the process of their call and understand what has been placed on the inside of them. This bride is the epitome of the church and it upsets God when its member parts go back in darkness and resubmits to the devil. The bill of divorce is said to have been instituted by Moses and given by God. However, Moses would not have done this unless he was instructed by God. This is supposedly characterized because the hardness of the hearts of mankind. This subject matter has very lucid and the veracity of its nature is truly a forgotten principle that is being used so loosely. The bible says in Isaiah 50:1, "Thus says the lord, where is the bill of your mother's divorcement, who I have put away" or which of my creditors is it to whom I have sold you?

Behold, for your iniquities have you sold yourselves, and for your transgressions is your mother put away. The writer has given a wider scope of the subject matter of divorce than we have for two people that were married. It is apparent that the meaning of divorces has a different implication than we can comprehend. Furthermore, the implication from Prophet Isaiah is that the meaning in the above mentioned scripture expands on the term divorce to the sentiments of child divorcing his mother. Far be it from the masses, this description here would characterize that putting away your mother is a form of divorcement.

The bible says in Matthew 5:32, "But I say unto you, That whosoever shall put away his wife, saving for the cause of fornication, causeth her to commit adultery: and whosoever shall marry her that divorced commiteth adultery.

Matthew gives the reader a comfort that implies that one who commits adultery or fornication is the only cause for consideration for divorce. In other words, Matthew has been sold on the sentiments that the only reason that is allowable is to find that your spouse has been unfaithful. There is wind of thinking that employs the notion that a spouse could acknowledge that it did happen but also take an opportunity to display mercy and forgive their spouse and continue to build in the relationship. The school of thought also indicated that abandonment is another example of a reason to divorce your spouse. Part of your responsibility as a spouse is to provide the essential level of intimacy.

In some circles, the abstaining spouse is held accountable for the inability to provide intimacy because of verbal abuse which makes the other spouse unable to be touched by the one conveying the abuse. The abused spouse is put in a position that hinders conjugal services are not being provided to the spouse living in the home that will stand on the word of God. The spouse who vacated the marriage is held to the highest court by abandoning him or herself from their god given provisions as a spouse. The fleshly choice to leave is the exiting spouse choice to move towards something greener on the other side. It might have been easy to see through the forest of opportunities in the days past. However, the chances of finding a mate without aides are slim to none. The selection process of going through a dating is so similar to a Pandora box. The skewed perspective is usually centered around an untamed spouse that has loosed lips for fleshly reasons. Most of the time, the struggle or frustration is a problem with money or bills.

In this area of marriage, many get divorced because of a lack of money and the burden of bills. When finances are lacking due to poor financial management or lack of funding, there is resounding effort the blame one another. Instead of regrouping to find who can handle money better, they decide to walk out of the union. It is an effort to talk at each other instead of talking with one another. While each spouse will use the blame game in effort to prove who is at fault, the central focus should be on seeking directions from the lord. In cases where both spouse are arguing without listening to the other spouse, this is a tool that the devil uses to divide the headship of the family. The new age view point of both being equal in terms of decision making has contributed to the down fall of the institution of marriage.

It is important for each spouse to allow the other spouse to be heard. This is a controversial issue with women who have control issues. Some feel that whoever makes the most money has an entitlement to be in authority. Although we are in a time with social issues, the role of husband and wife have never changed. God has given the man responsibility of headship and there are some misnomers in the area delegated duties. Some women feel that the men who delegate do it so they don't have to do it themselves. This is a profound error that the enemy has imputed in the mind of many women to feel qualified by the world standards attempt to take authority away from the man. Role reversal is nothing more than a movement the jezebel started in her effort to show other women how to make their men passive like Ahab. Needless to say, Jezebel's efforts have failed and the truth shall always make us free. The truth of God shall never change in terms of man-made agendas such as the pollution of the homosexual agenda to destroy the family structure in the way that God originally designed. The designer is totally upset with efforts of mankind to change his blue print.

CHAPTER 11
A CHEATERS DISCOURSE
THE INEVITABLE PATH TO DIVORCE.

The truth of a matter is that God is appalled at the lewd act's of mankind. Whether it be a pedophilers, a rape artists, fornicators, adulterers', God is not pleased with his creation. Because of free will, God is not surprised of the lawlessness and obnoxious behavior at the world in which he created. Although he did not want to make his creation controlled by him as if he were the puppet master, God chose to grant us the opportunity to make a choice to serve him by free will. In spite of his kindness and loyalty, God has been so good to those he created. While we live in a ungrateful society, the inhabitants of world feel as if they are entitled to the benefits in which he bestowed for those who live for him through a righteous lifestyle. Apparently, there is more to the balance scale between grace and the law required to access.

It is simply a matter of what was and now what is. Perhaps, this is what the devil desired to sabotage in order to bring confusion between those who attend church and those who are the church. The bridge has been torn down because of the nature of sin. Unfortunately, there are those who misunderstand the lingering effects of sins and to think that everyone should gain access to the pearly gates primarily because they are good people. The quest is not the issue but should be the norm for those who really desire to know him in an intimate manner. There are a various denominations that believe only in Calvinism, Hyper Calvinism, Monotheism, Polytheism or a host of other skewed views influenced by the mind set of religious theologians that gives us an open door policy.

In other words, they teach carnal principals that do not fall in line with the word of God. Some of these doctrines allow one to believe they will walk through the pearly gates without the remission of sins. In other words, the believer is entitled to live in a sin consciousness mindset that implies whatever sin they do is covered under the blood. Because the sting of death has been eradicated by Jesus Christ, many erroneous believers embrace the ideology there is no need to do anything because Jesus Christ has already paid the price. These poor souls have no clue of the sinners responsibility once they convert from the mindset of a sinner. The believer's lifestyle should reflect on the word of God and should be filled with his spirit. This ramification would counter the enemies' efforts and cause them to refrain from their lewd behavior. This behavior allows them to be better prepared and equipped relative to being armed with truth and danger against the enemies' tactics.

The enemy paints a portrait counterfeit righteousness where the saints can do the same things sinners do without any regards for judgment in the eyesight of God. Perhaps they believe that the all mighty God loves us to much to allow his creation to burn in the eternal flames of hell. The problem with this mindset is to develop a clear understanding of repentance. The sublime effort of some views as taught in the church is turn your situation around. However, the truth of the matter is that the church needs to run the opposite the directions from sin. Why do more Christians linger in sin? We realize that every born gain believer has a target on their chest. The devil and his imps' have launched an attack that will forever redefine warfare.

Moreover, there are those who have embraced the belief that attending church is the only requirement for access to heaven.

The church has many that attend church but does not understand to true meaning to become a part of this cosmic body. The time has come for the church to repent for not standing firmly on the word of God. Some churches have lowered their standards that anything goes on without fear God bring retribution to them. The bible clearly indicates that Eli allowed Hophna and Phineas to do ungodly and lewd acts in the temple. This same behavior has invaded the church without fear of God wrath. Not only does the church allow for lifestyles unbecoming to God to go on in the church there is not honor in representing God. The church can no longer use the "Thee I can't help it syndrome". The accountability to reverence God and the house of God has been abated to a level that indicates a tremendously falling away from the fear of God.

It is almost likened to the days when God removed his spirit from the temple. The nature of "Icobob" is a word used to imply the Glory of God has been removed. It is with contentment of the religious that believe that God will never forsake them nor leave them. This erroneous mindset is perpetuated on several poisonous doctrines interconnected with the devil that will hinder and destroy their ability to commune with the true and living God. Because of the specific design of man and woman, they were made to commune with one another. However, the devil and his worldly constituents have twisted the mindsets of millions who rather have sexual relations than to commune with God. In short, the spirit of lust has come to fruition and has been disseminated to the masses under their administration. Let us examine a scenario of a man carry a strong sexual addiction. He is a loving husband, family man, father and provider.

He is a man consumed with lust and often times will make an excuse for a unexpected business trips to cover up his agenda for sexual encounters. One day he has an encounter with the Lord and he confesses everything he has done to his wife. His wife is so distraught that she declares that she will do the same thing he has done. In a moment of rage, she declares that she will retaliate. Without thinking of the repercussions of her actions, she sets out a plan to get even. The devil has invaded marriages through a lust demon. This lust demon has gained access through various portals to create a great fall away from the true essence of marriage. In an effort to retaliate, some women have pledge to get even and go outside their marriage primarily because there mate has done likewise. The crack of infidelity has prompted many not to inform their spouse because they don't want to lose them in spite of their wrong doing.

One might say that what's good for the goose is good for the gander. It is profoundly perplexing to note that most of these cheaters do not want their spouse to cheat. It is a true saying that cheaters never prosper. When the spouse who is victimized by the cheating husband or vice versa, there is such profound hurt that is intertwined with anger and a determination to get even. The danger of this scenario is that feelings and bitterness develops and the focus to get even rises. The merit here is that no one is looking at the ramifications. Seeking revenged by essentially going to on the mission to cheat is a wrong response because you don't know the after effects. The first notion should be that it is an act against God and his word. The second notion is that it is act against your own flesh.

The third notion is that you step out of the will of God for the sake of revenge. The husband had cheated against his vows that he made between God and his wife. The devil uses the gateways of doubt to gain entrance into the lives of believers. However, the wife may go out to get her revenge and could end up with a life threatening disease or possibly get pregnant in the journey for revenge. More importantly, she might seek vengeance and loose her soul. This decision could perhaps be more dangerous than the feelings inherited by the marital violation. It is easy to look at this situation and make a feudal decision to divorce your spouse or you could display mercy just as the Lord spoke to Gomer about Hosea. Although the word of God is very precise in terms of evil versus good, there is a strong line of deference in a person making a mistake with sin and one who practices sin.

The old adage that conveys this message, "Once a cheater always a cheater." Despite the principles applied in these old adages, there is always a chance for good to come out of anyone that chooses to trust & walk with God. Many feel that they are walking with God but they really only know about him because of what a member of the family such as Grandma has told them. This generation of believers fail to get up close and tight with God because they don't think living holy and righteous is exciting. They erroneously assumed that time will wait on them so they can continue to have a little more fun. The clock is progressively ticking and the soon return of the father to embrace his bride is the full manifestation of true marriage. While this is so important and true, there is no time like to now to be on the right side and walk in an intimate relationship with the true and awesome God.

The religious circles have assumed that hearing the word of God and being in attendance gives you access to heavenly benefit's. There are multitudes that attend church on a regular basis and do not have a personal relationship with God. The current mindset of people is likened to a current crack addict. They feel like coming to the church to get a quick fix and then go out the door look to engage in previous unsavory patterns. This behavior has infiltrated in the church in such a manner that one would see the church as a mirage. In other words, too many people embrace a warped expression of the church and never gain the experience in true worship. Religion has perpetuated a false sense of worship with regard to church attendance. The mere jester to think that coming to church is your only obligation.

Living in the sin-field world is the biggest test because God entrust that each born again believer will live righteously in order to be part of his bride. God has invested too much of himself into the every born again believer to allow the effects of sin to marvel at the image of the bride he is awaiting with great splendor and anticipation. He awaits the manifestation of the bride to come forth in spite of the efforts of the delegated authority granted to the devil by the God. This is purely incomprehensible to the average church members because they are not aware of the intricacies of righteousness. The commitment that God has to the church is impoverished because he sees the perfected image. However, the model for marriage one earth is skewed because there are no perfect couples. Even in the eyes of Hosea, he was distraught because Gomer decided to go back into the life of prostitution.

Can you imagine the sentiments of Hosea when God told him to go get her and bring his wife back home. The instructions by God to Hosea is not only admirable because he took God at his word. However, there are wondering minds that contends that her struggle with the life of prostitution and being Hosea's wife would continue to surround trust. Every time Gomer went out the house, Gomer had to be stressed that she might revisit the life of prostitution. The soul tie is in this case a dagger type of spiritual connection that lingers in the life of people who have engage in sexual exploitation. God used the example of Gomer and Hosea to epitomize the relationship with Israel who wandered away from Gods love. While the entire clan of people knew about Gomer's affairs, it must have

assimilated God relationship with Israel. In spite of Gomers efforts to win her back, she ran off with those lovers who promised her great wealth and things that gave her enjoyment. Gomer did not share the love of Hosea's God and revolted back in the life in which she was content. She left her children to live out the desire of her flesh. It is the same today, more people are in love with material possession and wealth. Just as Hosea longed for Gomer to come home, God has the same longer for his creation to come home with him.

CHAPTER 12
WHEN GOD REFUSES TO HEAR THE PRAYERS OF A HUSBAND AND WIFE?

The bible declares in James 5:16, "Confess your faults one to another and pray one for another, that ye may be healed. The effectual fervent prayers of the righteous man availeth much. The bible is clearly conveyed by James to share that the believers should be open enough to convey faults to each other as they engage in the journey of righteousness. It is important to note that there is a wisdom that should be considered with you are dealing with something in the serious nature that should only be shared with those of maturity and those in leadership. The danger of sharing serious things is to be cautioned by those who are just entering in the family of the Lord. The wisdom approach of sharing too much with novices could trigger a relapse into Satan's kingdom. The purpose of this text by James is let those who come in the family know that there are going to be times where mistakes will be made.

Many have confused a mistake with basically premeditated sin. The power of agreement is a strong tool for those who connect in the kingdom. The battle has continued to brew between light and darkness. The enemy has always slid through a crack or portal of the lives of those who pursue righteousness. It is the very essence of darkness to set back and wait for the opportunity to enter into the lives of the righteous because access has been granted. One of the hidden mysteries of marriage is the ability to keep the devil out of its sphere of influence. The strategy of the enemy should keep in mind that the serpent beguiled eve in the Garden of Eden. As a reminder, the enemy is always looking for an access point or gateway to infiltrate its effort to sow discord. The platform of marriage should not be considered a venue for the enemy to infiltrate.

The relationship between a husband and wife should be impenetrable by the enemy. If the enemy can continue to keep the purity of matrimony at bay, he will assume that true intimacy shall not be met. The direct mission of the devil is to create havoc and to hinder all efforts of believers from pursuing righteousness. When a believer is bombarded with attacks from the enemy, the defensive efforts have been broken through the veil. This frontal attack is normally contingent on the believer's preparation to engage in warfare. Consequently, the initial plateau is in the area of prayer life. When the prayer life of a believer has been hindered or halted, the enemy launches an attack to overthrow. During the attack, the enemy may not get the one who has a strong prayer life. However, he will endeavor to pursue someone in the household to keep the believer aware that the enemy has made a negative impact.

On the other hand, the enemy will get closer by hitting a bulls eye on the husband or wife. In order for prayer to fruitful, the incumbents must maintain direct contact in their prayer life. This approach will prevent the believers from have dull sensory. In other words, the incumbents will still be able to hear clearly. The ability to hear from God by every believer should be their quest. Moreover, the ability to hear became dull to the point where the believer could no longer hear from God. This should be a wakeup call to all who have a genuine and authentic relationship with God. This is innate ability is given to his creations once they have accepted Jesus Christ as their Lord and Savior.

Part of the acceptance of what we now know as salvation, the new believer has renounced Satan and their allegiance to him. Each candidate for marriage must realize that Satan is angry at God and angry at himself for allowing the candidate to slip through his hands.

Nevertheless, the damage has been done and now the believer must reconnect to the ultimate source before it is too late. The devil uses this tactic to invade the candidates for marriage through the soulish realm. It is this realm where individuals react according to the flesh and their feelings. Many marriages are entered based on their current feelings and they do not know how to approach God because they don't have a relationship. There are many marriages that were entered based off of loneliness and lust. Unfortunately, they were tricked to think that once they appeased their flesh everything else would line up. According to I Corinthian 10:13, "There hath no temptation taken you but such as is common to man: but God is faithful, who will not suffer you to be tempted above that ye are able: but will with the temptation also make a way to escape, that ye may be able to bear it."

Apostle Paul initially depicts that no temptation hath taken you, but such as is common to man. The human frailty to expect good from men of such principles as heathens and such power or resolution that mere men could bear you through is not possible in the eyesight of God. Men and women may be false and the world full of sin but God is faithful. God knows what we can bear, and what we cannot bear up against. The bible says in I Peter 3:7,"Likewise, ye husbands, dwell with them according to knowledge, giving honour unto the wife, as unto the weaker vessel, and as being heirs together of the grace of life, that your prayers be not hindered. The apostle gives a discourse as to dwelling with the wife according to knowledge. He further emphasized that the dwelling should not be according to lust nor according to passion but according to knowledge as a wise and sober man of the word of God.

The Apostle further instructs the believing husband to give honor to their wife by giving her respect, allowing her to operate in her delegated authority and protecting her from harm and danger. He furthermore admonishes men to trust their wives and delighting in conversation with her. In other words, God did not want men to treat them like brutish savages with passions of devils. He wanted them to be respected, supported and honored. Apostle Peter, more or less, emphasized acutely that the wives were the weaker vessels and should be honored as equal vessels to her husband. The focus for every marriage should be earmarked to be heirs together of the grace of life. The missing link in many marriages seems to be the connection piece to the one who created he them and the institution of marriage.

Many husbands treat their wives as second class citizens or indentured slaves. Instead of looking at their wives as equal in the eye sight of God, there seems to be a missing link of the divine order. The Yoke is a device that is used by an ox to keep him in alignment. The Yoke also represents a device for submission. Although the ox is a tremendously strong animal, the Yoke keeps him in alignment. While others may think it is bondage, there is a true sense of liberty as it relates to righteousness. It is amazing that God does not put a yoke on believers to keep them in alignment. The bible says in Jeremiah 27:2-4, "Thus saith the Lord unto me: Make thee bonds and yokes, and put them upon thy neck, And send them to the King of Edom, and to the King of Moab, and to the King of the Ammorites, and to the King of Tyrus, and to the King of Zidon, by the hand of the messengers which come to Jerusalem unto Zedekiah king of Judah.

The Lord spoke to Prophet Jeremiah in the Jeremiah 27 to make the yoke out of leather straps and wooden crossbars and to put it on his neck. From this biblical example, all who engage in marriage should declare a public declaration of dependence. That is, a dependence on God and not flesh. The plans of mankind have hindered the world to the point there is a drastic difference of marriage in the world and in the church. The surrendering aspect of each candidate would require each to give up their person ideology of marriage and accept the plans of God. Upon surrendering, both parties are totally submitted to Jesus Christ. Now they have given their lives to him and took up his yoke. The responsibilities are no longer their but now belong to Jesus Christ. This drafted pattern is suppose to be the blue print for believers to embrace. The bible says in 2 Corinthians 6:14, "Be ye not unequally yoked together with unbelievers for what fellowship hath righteousness with unrighteousness? And what communion hath light with darkness?

Apostle Paul has give us a clear directive not to be yoke together with unbelievers. Why is there such a pull for those in the light to be drawn to those in darkness. All throughout society, it is clearly evident that many good girls find themselves pulled toward those boys who are labeled bad. While the same scripture reference above, Apostle Paul also shares that believers and unbelievers should not have fellowship with one another. In a strict sense, believers and unbelievers should not set to a table and one another's house to break bread. This seems to be a drastic approach to building friends or to develop kingdom relationship. In other words, this segment of scripture gives a power directive that light and dark should not be intertwined.

With that being said, two people from different religious faith would not have a chance of making it together in a marital relationship because of it is forbidden. If it is forbidden on this level, how could their being level of communication one with another between those in the church and those in the world? How does one work in conditions where there must be communication? Are these forbidden scenarios that caution society to avoid any level of interaction. This misconception between communing and communication is extremely different. When two individuals communicate, there is only an exchange of information. The information is transmitted in both directions but there is not clear cut relationship established. The exchange of information can never be accepted as communing because one person decides to talk to another.

When a sinner decides to changes their life, they begin to pray to ask God for forgiveness of their sins in order gain access to God for a closer relationship. The religious mindset says that they talk to God all the time and pray to him as well. It is at this point of the process where the religious individual does not comprehend the requirements to gain access. The unheralded belief that every creature has been saved through the death and burial of Jesus Christ is saved. Salvation is plan and process where the lines of communication can be restored in you only embrace Jesus Christ as your Lord and Savior. Through this process, the unbeliever can now embrace Jesus Christ as their personal savior and have access to the benefit of righteousness. One of the precious benefits of every believer is to have access to the heavenly father which is only attained through Jesus Christ.

The Holy Spirit is our guide and comforter who serves as a third portion of the triuneness of God. This third member of the Godhead is our intercessor to the father and has a unique ability to enter into every believer as an invited guest. He begins to communicate and commune to the father on your behalf. The amazing qualities of the Holy Spirit is to serve as an advocate of heaven to speak through your spirit when you have reach your highest peak. In other words, every believer takes a journey through a feverish desire to gain access to the father. In this journey, the human side becomes faint and through head knowledge begins to get exhausted and drained. It is during these times that the Holy Spirit intervenes and takes it to another level on the believers behalf. Through this in comprehensible abilities to act on all believers behalf, the Holy Spirit enables the believer to access a dimension of heaven that is paralleled to the quagmire of pleasures of the wealthiest people in the word. This unprecedented ability is often unrealized those who do have access granted. The ability to hear God should be treasured to all who have been granted access by way of the Holy Spirit.

This provision is only merited by Gods best for everyone who embraces him through the divine relationship in which has earmarked for his Children. After all, what father would not want the good pleasure to commune with his Children.

CHAPTER 13
THE JAGGED EDGE OF REMARRIAGE AFTER THE DEATH A SPOUSE.

It is such a shame that many people think that there is one template for the institution of marriage. What works for one person house-hold may not work in another person's home? There are many factors that can enable or disable marriage. Every marriage is different and it is important not to assume that the every candidate will respond to the same challenges in the same manner. As difficult as it is to make two people to become one, there is no easy recipe for a successful marriage. However, if Christ is in the center of a marriage, the chances are much higher that the marriage will be successful. It takes an extreme amount of work to make a marriage flow smoothly. The discouragement of marriages in our modern day venue is that connecting with a spouse that balances one another. It is simply a severing of a coin or a reconnection of a coin has unique application. The same discouragement continues to be conveyed in the area of remarriages as well.

The bible says in Nehemiah 7:1-3, "Now it came to pass, when the wall was built, and I had set up the doors, and the porters and the singers and the Levites were appointed, That I gave my brother Hanani, and Hananiah the ruler of the palace, charge over Jerusalem: for he was a faithful man, and feared God above many. And I said unto them, Let not the gates of Jerusalem be opened until the sun be hot; and while they stand by, let them shut the doors, and bar them appoint watches of the inhabitants of Jerusalem, everyone in his watch, and every one to be over against his house. Now the city was large and great; but the people were few therein, and the houses were not built"

The sentiments of Nehemiah can be applied in the aspect of marriages and remarriages. The wall built based on previous marriages could be a hindrance to the new or present marriage. The gate or gateway to your past or past memories can be detrimental to the new marriage. The new house shall not be built based on the foundation of the previous relationship. In spite of how the relationship ended be it death or divorced, there is definitely a need for a new plan to build the house without elements from the past. The modern day view would categorize this gate as baggage from the past. The difficult task is the human ability to sift through the pain and the good times without reflecting on the current marriage. In other words, the previous relationship could have been beautiful and the tendency to talk to your spouse in the midst of comparing the two is truly an unfair assessment.

In light of death being the culprit of a marriage ending, there must be time for healing. Sometimes, the memories will be lingering into the new relationship. As unfair as this may be, the need for some type of counseling may need to take place before the candidate enters into a new marriage. In every case, healing wounds may be so deep that the new spouse may need to be patient before entering into this new covenant relationship. The rise in relationship which may have ended in death by the hand of the other spouse is an indication to proceed with caution. This pattern was traditionally kept a secret but now has come to the surface. New information is on the rise of physical & mental abuse among women that have been enslaved in this addictive and controlling type of relationship. The fear to leave and the threat of being killed has negatively conditioned more women to stay in relationships that should have been ended.

If the threat is taken seriously, the fear of the abusive spouse to harm the children is always at risk. The mindsets of some philosophers, theologians and other experts will say that the victims are not necessarily excused from their marital covenant. In this case, this writer gives you an excuse to tell the devil that you are not going to hell. There is tendency to become legalistic in the sense that their spouse has some mental issues and he needs medical attention. This behavior has always been recorded in the world, but now it has slipped into the corridors of the church. Although the gap of abuse exist on both sides of the coin, the margin of abuse extends much greater towards the women. This is not to excuse any of this behavior whether it is a jezebel or Ahab spirit involved. The spirit of the latter is not geared toward gender. It is a false tendency to assume that the jezebel is only for woman or Ahab is only for men.

The men who have been abused are too ashamed to mention this because of the ridicule of other men. Unfortunately, the statistics are not able to be adequately assessed because more men are not reporting. Because the rampant rate of divorce, there is another issue that should be considered in the matter of remarriage. The issue of blending the children and /or does your ensuing spouse desire to have the responsibility of your children. There are cases where some women will desire a man to be responsible in financial sense but not in the matter of discipline. There are cases where some men fall in love with the woman but does not desire to have the children live with them. This particular type of man encourages to give the children to their father. What kind of woman would give up her children for a man? It is obvious that this man if not carrying the characteristics of Christ. There are many good men that may or may not have six figure salaries, big jobs or professional athletes.

Some of these men embrace Christian women through marriage and have embraced their children. In other words, this Christian woman had several children that resulted in child rearing prior to accepting Jesus Christ. The men, on the other hand, may have had some children during their worldly walk. Although many of these men did not play a role in their children's lives nor did the women require them. These women accepted the responsibility of their action with these men and released them. However, God did not release them to from there seed. The recompense for this negligence will haunt them forever. The renovation of the minds of these fathers will endeavor to reach out to those neglected children to be friends only if they would accept them.

It is through the power of God that men are reclaiming their seed and repenting for neglecting them. Some children refuse to allow a relationship to be built based off of the pain of not being in their lives when they needed them. There are some men who have not sought forgiveness from their children nor God for taking care of another man's children but neglected them in the process. Aside from this pain in their pit, these men have found forgiveness by the God they now serve. However, the rare jewel of a man does not section off the children to only the one he shared in creating. The veracity of parenting can be a perplexing concept with new marriages. Depending on status and role of the biological parent, there can be some extreme circumstances. The issue of faith in the custodial parent's house has been fermented by that house in which they live.

On another note, the biological parent is more open with religion and instructs his child to open up his minds to embrace other religions. This disposition can create an intense problem with the whole parenting process for the Christian family. The issue becomes a household one where the child will be torn in their belief because one parent believes in one faith and the other believes in another. Some may view this as a matter of choice. The gateway for demons to gain access into a household has now been established. During the process of preparing for the a marriage, it is important to do a background check on your prospective mate. In order to get a better idea of your spouse, you should have three distinct areas of consideration. The first area of concern should be a criminal background to see what if any type of criminal activity that candidates have been involved. How long were they involved? Are they currently involved in that life style? Did they do any time in prison? If so, what was the reason for going to prison?

It is important that you have an idea of the nature of the crime because it could have detrimental effects on your life. In retrospect, each candidate should know the nature of the crime. Does the candidate have the propensity to revisit that nature? Was the candidate a serial killer, rapist, bank robber, pedophile, child pornographer? This is the best time to allow your imagination to run wild because you will ultimately be sleeping in the bed with this person. The second area of concern should be a credit check to see how this person has handled their financial credibility. Does this person know how to balance a check book? Does this person have the means to financially contribute to the household budget? Who will handle the finances? Which mate is better enabled to keep the household finances in line? Determine the communication barriers for finances, spending protocols, savings? Does your mate have any financial obligation such as child support? If so, how many children? What type of savings plan should the family establish?

Develop college savings for the Children? How many credit cards to keep and maintain between the two? Does this person make efforts to plan for vacations? There are a host of question that should be personalized according to each particular situation. Give yourself a chance to choose whether or not you want to deal with a person who has an adverse past. At least, you will have a better understanding of the person that you have this potential relationship. This pattern of assessment will also afford you a chance to see if the candidate is honest enough to lay all the cards on the table.

The third area of concern should be an Aides Test. This is a major concern particularly if you have a high propensity to live a biblical life. The sex after marriage clause will at least allow you to know that the person was will to wait and that they understood your convictions for wanting to be celibate until the wedding night. Although each candidate may have been married or this may be the first time, the life threatening disease has already taken millions of lives for living a promiscuous lifestyle. It is apparent that some choose to use contraceptives because they believe in the try it before they get marriage reasoning in the scope of compatibility. The logic behind this violation of Gods plan for marriage is futile at best because God did not intend for intimacy between a husband and wife to be compatible or comparable. This attitude and logic is best assessed the invasion of sexual promiscuity. The essence of intimacy for one spouse to another should not be base on a world expression of sexual intimacy. The devil has disguised love making by releasing it very sexual nature that does not carry any level of intimacy. The nature of this sexual exploitation is purely a quest to secure notches on your belt as to how many sexual encounters the candidate has had. The connection is based more of releasing his nature into another as a form of conquest or to solidify his manhood. This attitude and conduct is truly a deviation of the plan in which God has for the true nature of divine intimacy. Some people would rather be by themselves rather than just having a mate to express their sexual excursions.

IN SUMMARY

In Summary, the book entitled, What Do You Do When You Marry the Wrong Rib? Coming From A Place Called There! is a book that many have questions but no answers as to why there are so many people who have been married but ended up in a divorce. Why are there so many divorces coming forth? Why do people get married to the wrong persons? Were there any signs that could have prevented them from getting married. Peer pressure in the church has been a problem because the leaders desire the members to be family based.

AUTHOR'S REFLECTION

Kenneth D. Grimble is a prophetic and apostolic strategist in this end time season of the Lord. This book entitled, "What Do You Do When You Marry the Wrong Rib? Coming From A Place Called There! is a journey down the road of despair for me because it cautioned each married couple to ask why did you marry your mate. Marriage is not an amusement park nor should it be taken lightly. Some have chosen to treat marriage like a series of carnival rides that people continue get off one and get on another one for a ride. Instead many find that they have positioned themselves to get on the ride and then find that they don't like the ride so they get off. Marriage is much more than a ride in an amusement park. God requires a serious commitment and mandates a vow in matrimony This institution was not designed as a play ground of pleasure. God is asking the same question with all of the believer who say they love him but are unwilling to live without him. Regardless of what you think about the subject matter, the writer and the message in this book is not telling anyone to go out to divorce there mate. However, this book should be a prerequisite for anyone desiring to get married and those desiring to building a stronger marriages. Dr. Kenneth D. Grimble is happily married to Lady Diane Grimble, the apple of his eye.

www.ingramcontent.com/pod-product-compliance
Lightning Source LLC
LaVergne TN
LVHW051508080426
835509LV00017B/1987